Wildfire Weeds

Mori Natura

ISBN (Print Edition): 978-1-54397-361-7

ISBN (eBook Edition): 978-1-54397-362-4

Dear Cindy,

To all the homesteaders!

WILD
FIRE
WEEDS

MORI NATURA

With love,
Mori Natura

PROLOGUE

Marijuana, like all plants, knows the magic of photosynthesis. After mixing the elements of warming sunshine, friable earth, fresh water, and carbon dioxide together, a seed may grow into a towering giant within a few months. As a seed, cannabis offers incredible nutrition; gather enough seeds and one can press a nutritious and life-giving oil. Let the seed grow, and you have a plant that provides durable material for fiber, which can then be made into rope, clothing, or paper. There are few plants as utilitarian as cannabis. However, if left to mature to fruition, marijuana has the unique ability to produce an intoxicating matrix of hairs and crystals. In truth, we draw our backdrop from here in the garden, with the cannabis plant, full of glory and ready to be harvested on the ridge top of Redwood Valley in Mendocino County. After a summer of being cared for, a stand of herbs rooted in the earth reaches to the heavens with a bouquet of mind-altering flowers flourishing in the airy realms between. Human minds work to breed the seeds for optimal production, human hands help to ensure careful tending, and human breath offers a delicious food for the plants to succeed. All across Northern California, October features marijuana plants nourished by human exhalations in the fullness of their life cycle. Symbiotically connected, humans then breathe in the marijuana plant that they have been so invested in cultivating. And so begins our tale.

CHAPTER 1

Monday October 2, 2017

Morning

"The flowers are beautiful this morning! I think we've got another fine crop out back. Won't be long now before the rest is ready to hang up and dry. The 'OG Strawberry' seems fit to burst!" Spruce removed his work gloves and placed them on the kitchen counter. He had spent the wee hours of the work day checking on the various strains they were cultivating in their pot patch.

Willow was stirring her tea at the kitchen table. She nodded as he spoke.

"What's for breakfast?" Spruce sat down at the table, ready to join his wife in planning out their day.

"Canna-Smoothie and granola." Willow mouthed the words but she was looking out the window, distracted.

Their kitchen window opened their cabin home wide onto the outside world. From the purview of their kitchen table, they could see the entire rolling hills landscape stretched out before them. Often they could see the local wildlife making their trails across the terrain, but today there wasn't much movement in the distance. Only the feathered flourishing of the morning birds singing to the sun in the trees was heard. The dawn was still, and Willow wasn't watching the theater of the wild scenery play out so much as allowing the brightening sunlight to mesmerize her as it fell on the golden California hills, illuminating another day.

Meanwhile, Spruce plunged into his granola bowl. The granola had been made from oats that they had grown themselves in the garden, then sliced by a hand-cranked roller mechanism and baked to perfection with nuts and seeds in their solar oven. The smoothie had been blended using home-cultured kefir, fruits from their trees, and green leaves from a patch of young cannabis plants they kept in the greenhouse expressly for use in the kitchen as a food. When Willow finally came out of her reverie, she said, "We need to cut down the grasses around the property again."

"Yes. I've put it off long enough. You're right. I'll get out there today and start taking the grasses down," Spruce said and smiled before scooping up another bite of granola with his spoon.

Willow finally looked at him. "It feels bone dry out there, Spruce." At the sound of his name, Spruce's gaze shifted up to take in his anxious wife, fingering her teacup but not eating or drinking anything.

Indeed, it was as dry as ever. October usually meant rain was coming, and the homesteaders could start lighting up their wood stoves for warmth once the land was saturated with a good soaking rain.

"At least the crop benefits from a dry fall," Spruce added between bites.

Which was true: Willow knew that once the rains began, the pot harvest was a wild commotion aimed at mold mitigation and frantically getting the flowers hanging to dry before the moisture damaged the buds. Rains late in the fall meant that there was going to be a lot of extra work setting up tarps and sloshing about haphazardly to protect the dense flower colas from too much wetness.

"Yes, I suppose you're right," she said. "Just be sure to get the grass down in the meadow today, ok?" Willow looked directly into Spruce's eyes as she said this.

Finishing his last bite of granola, Spruce took up his bowl and spoon, walked to the sink, and said "I'm on it, honey!" After he washed his bowl, Spruce Wilder strode out to his workshop.

Willow Wilder kept staring outside. The golden shades were now pronounced in distinct tiers of hills, all leading up to their kitchen window where the elevation peaked and the surrounding land could be seen for miles and miles. She was musing about evacuation plans. Her fears had absorbed her since July, when a fire had started on the nearest highway. A car engine had exploded into flames while trekking up the grade, a steep climbing stretch of the U.S. highway 101 that connected the small cities of Ukiah and Willits. The vehicle had erupted into flames that quickly whipped up the fuel-filled ridge of dry grasses, turning the hillside from golds to reds and then to browns and blacks and whites as the fire burned to ash. She had sat at that same window that July afternoon watching huge columns of smoke billowing up into the sky like a volcano purging fiery smoke into the heavens. As ash rained down she had feared for her home, wondering if those hot ashes would fall down onto their property's expanse of dry grasses with just enough coal left in them to start a blaze. Midsummer in Northern California was the high time for a wildfire to break loose. Looking over the hillside, she knew that it would only take one good spark to set the tinder box landscape aflame. Every summer she watched the sky turn to smoky grey as fires claimed more and more of the land within a 100-mile radius of her home. This summer the blaze had been too close; she settled uneasily into her chair, musing on the danger of no rain in October in California.

Spruce, however concerned he may have been with the fire on the highway, had felt that the scare in July had come and gone and that they had survived the fire season yet another year. Lightning doesn't strike twice, does it? They both experienced a deep fear when they watched the smoke rising up that summer day. Where they had been afforded complacency before the July incident, they committed themselves to more fire management than ever before after they saw how close a fire had come to their homestead. For two months they had been more sensitive to the needs of the land surrounding their home; they made a plan of action to protect their home, and they were doing their best to make time to carry out their intentions.

Although he was not completely ambivalent about the threat of fire, Spruce was more focused on cultivating pot than Willow. He had a crop to bring in, and he had spent the bulk of the summer stewarding his backyard agricultural endeavor. He had spent the last thirty years farming his annual weed crop from seed to flower. Despite some anxiety that came to mind with regard to poorly timed wildfires breaking out, the demands of his livelihood took primary focus in his mind. And so he whistled when he took out his scythe from his workshop and headed out to the meadow to keep the grasses cut back. It was too late in the year to use the mower; one errant spark could change their lives forever.

"MMMMMEEAAAAAA!" Came the call from the barn. The goats were ready to be milked. Willow gathered her bucket of kitchen scraps and headed out to the animals, who lived in a barn building adjacent to their cabin. Next she opened the chicken coop. The hens circled about her feet, clucking contentedly in anticipation of their morning breakfast. She offered them sprouted grains and a bucket of green weeds she had harvested the night before from the garden. The mixture included herbs such as comfrey, purslane, and dandelion that thrived in the well-watered food garden. Grasses and other green things that volunteered in the garden beds were carefully removed to be fed to the hens. Willow scattered the kitchen scraps outside the coop, and the hens took off toward them. As they scratched apart the greens looking for choice bug morsels to eat while shredding the big leaves to bits, Willow went into the protected center of the coop where the nesting boxes were carefully built so as to withstand predatory attacks in the night. Slowly, delicately, she harvested the eggs from their straw nests, many of them still warm to the touch. Six eggs with rich orange yolks were the perfect base to make a free-range frittata, a local flavor quiche, or a homegrown omelet for the couple's meals.

Willow left the coop feeling slightly more optimistic. The animals always had a way of changing her mood for the better. Even when they got out in the garden or misbehaved, she had to smile at the love she felt for these barnyard charges she had taken into her care; they grounded her and helped her feel connected to the land and gardens around her property.

As Willow approached the stanchion, the cries from the goats rose to a loud and ardent bawl. The jig was up. She had been seen, and the three lady goats all filed into place to be milked. She opened the pen and out ran Thistle before she closed the barn gate. With agility and precision Thistle leaped and bounded from stall to stanchion, jumping into place, shoving her head between the holding posts, and looking Willow in the eyes while bleating to be fed her special milking treats without further ado; please and thank you! From a large aluminum can, Willow grabbed a cup full of acorns and laid these on the bottom of the stanchion feeding trough. On top of these, she added some sprouted grains and greens; similar yummies had been distributed to the chickens. Occasionally, she added some seaweed that they had harvested on their trips to the beach as a super powder for her salty lasses.

While Thistle dove into her breakfast, Willow entered the small dairy kitchenette that occupied the western corner of the barn. There she procured a milking bucket, a warm wet cloth, glass jars, and a funnel with a filter fitted into it. Upon returning, Willow started singing to Thistle an acapella piece that she improvised riffs on every day during milking. She positioned the bucket in place, washed down Thistle's udder, and squeezed off two squirts of milk, one from each teat, to clear the passageway. Before long, Willow was singing at full volume, the goats were all milked, the chickens were scratching the dirt for bugs, and the day had sincerely begun on the homestead.

Spruce carefully took his scythe down from the barn wall. He sharpened the blade in small circles, letting the whetstone make the curved line ready to pierce through the dried grasses in the fields. He had mowed around the house early in the spring as they attempted to create a defensible space to protect. It came with the territory that they would do whatever they could to protect against the threat of fire. They used portable fencing to create grazing areas for the goats and chickens, who kept the brush down all around the house. But Willow had been getting at Spruce to clear the more distant areas leading up to their homestead. The later the year rode on and the sun shone high and the grasses dried, the more Willow pleaded with Spruce to take his yard maintenance to the next level. There wasn't so much the fear of a fire in his mind as the certainty that fire would come. It felt obvious on some intrinsic level: California had a relationship with fire and that ecological bond would continue forever.

Spruce had studied with some of the local Native Americans in the area. He had felt drawn to their traditions, knowledge, and reverence for nature. Spruce remembered his first meeting with a Pomo elder, whose tribe had lived in Mendocino County for countless generations. He enrolled in a workshop taught by the elder on sustainable land use the same year that he bought property in the hills of Redwood Valley. The encounter forged new pathways in Spruce's mind, and he deeply appreciated learning about the place where he had put down roots for his family. From that day forty years ago Spruce dedicated himself to creating a viable and symbiotic relationship with the land. Acknowledging his own inherited colonial ancestry of so called "settlers" who had unjustly claimed land already inhabited by indigenous populations for themselves, Spruce attempted to mitigate the harm of his predecessors by integrating local knowledge into his land management practices. He felt more kinship with cultural ethics that valued the protection and preservation of the environment. He wasn't sure how the world could return to a version of cooperative ecological conservation where people came together to collectively and thoughtfully value caring for the land. However, he had poured over innumerable talks and books describing the stewardship practices of the Northern California tribes who had once lived sustainably on the land. Looking for a way to understand the earth beneath his feet, Spruce returned again and again to the indigenous knowledge of California's ecosystems. For him, nothing fascinated his intellect more than the education he received from the people who had lived successfully, thriving in concert with nature for thousands of years.

As he hiked down to the meadows that needed thinning, his scythe over his left shoulder, he thought about the exotic and invasive grasses he was about to cut down. The dew was still clinging to the grasses as he walked; the golden stalks stood firm, even though precious moisture had collected along the heavy seed heads over the course of the cool evening. As he hoisted down his tool, the appointed grim reaper of golden grasses wondered when the native grasses had died and these grassy weeds had taken over? Certainly, cattle ranching in the Wild West brought more aggressive, invasive species of grasses, forever changing the face of the California landscape. These annual grasses had shallow roots; they were not intended to be part of the California landscape; they were not able to help assuage drought, mitigate wildfire damage, or preserve the ecosystems that had thrived here for so long. It would take a heavy rain to weigh these adamant grass stalks down.

A deluge would soften and collapse them back to the earth, as they became food for the next chapter. Spruce lived to watch the eternal play of the landscape enacted across the stage of the seasons. Fall particularly juxtaposed the abundance of the land, the height of fruition, and the celebration of cultivation with the death phase at the end of the cycle. California's unrelenting summer sun would have her way time and time again. Fierce heat would stifle and sap the life force from the plants whose glory had just been realized. They, too, would fall and dissolve into a mulched end of times. The apocalypse came yearly to the hills of California. Even though the weight of the rains would gradually shove the dead grass shoots back to the earth for their terrestrial burial, their covering of the earth would help other things come alive. Mycelium proliferated in their white webs, casting up mushrooms as a memorial of the summer grasses, and the fallen seeds had a chance to sprout again with the renewed moisture, bringing along with them wildflowers and tree seedlings reaching toward the warmth of the sun. When the days turned short and the heat became more welcome than overwhelming, a genesis of life signaled rebirth on the forest floor. By ending the grassy sentinels' journey to the heavens, the rains marked the beginning of a moist, lush renaissance.

This morning, the heat of the day had yet to consume Spruce; he tested the cutting edge of his tool in the full fall sunshine. Confidently, he sharpened the scythe's blade on his whetstone until he believed his tool would achieve a smooth swishing motion to temper the tall grassy world. But he knew it wasn't enough of a defense. If fires came to their land, the land would still be too dry. He knew that his efforts were symbolic and perfunctory at best. Against an actual wildfire, their homestead of wooden construction could serve as fuel for the flames. But he prepared his scythe to slice on anyway. Besides, he would gather the straw after he felled it and use it for projects in the gardens. He silently debated with himself about whether it would be more beneficial to use the straw for building material for a new structure or if realistically he only had the time to apply it as mulch over his garden beds.

Spruce put in his earphones and listened to a podcast about wildfire management and fire suppression techniques as applied by the native Californians. He'd been thinking about this more and more lately, and he had hours of toil before him that presented the perfect opportunity for his curious leanings to brood on different methodologies. With that, he loosed the scythe so that it sliced through the first patch of gold.

Willow led the goats on a short walk to a field where they pastured on whatever they could find. At this time of the year it wasn't much. They nibbled a bit of manzanita here, some Himalayan blackberry hedges there, and they would in all likelihood spend the rest of the day in whatever shade they could find, rubbing their heads against trees to scratch goaty itches that welled up from within their capricious souls.

Willow brought the goat milk in from the barn and used a portion of it to feed her kefir culture which lived on her kitchen counter. Kefir, yogurt's cousin of mysterious origins, feeds off lactose to firm up milk in a delicious and simple way. Willow had experimented with many ways of fermenting, and she found that having a daily pint of kefir kept her culture thriving in her kitchen and her own digestion pleased as well. Daily after milking she used a wooden spoon to scoop out the pile of kefir culture "grains" to add to the day's fresh milk. They weren't really grains at all but had been dubbed grains by laypeople who were not savvy to fermentation science. In Willow's opinion, the so-called grains resembled ivory brains. In fact, these fermenting architects of the kefir community wove a complex symbiotic super-organism. Combining bacteria and yeast, kefir consumed sweet dairy sugars to produce a particularly pleasing culture. By the next morning, her milk had become a probiotic kefir elixir, ready to consume, and the kefir grains were ready to be refreshed. Occasionally she would be busy or forgetful of her billions of probiotic pets in the kitchen, and they would so thoroughly digest the goat milk that when she resumed her maternal duties as a culturer she would be left with her kefir grains floating in a kefir cheese curd pile atop a solution of whey. Little Miss Muffet style, Willow knew how to use her over-fermented products. The kefir cheese served as a soft spread in her meals for the day. The whey could be used to further other ferments along as an enzymatic catalyst for the fermentation of beverages and vegetables and for tenderizing meats. Diverging from her nursery rhyme counterpart, for Willow, spiders in the country were emblems of a land-based livelihood. Rather than be frightened by their presence throughout her kitchen and home, she considered them decorative elements. Arachnid webs mirrored back the technological advances of the natural world, and she was pained by the idea of sweeping away their silken masterpieces. Occasionally, Willow would let a ferment go on for far too long, and that smell elicited a frightful response; as the milk soured past edibility, her fermented dairy science experiment manufactured an audacious aroma. Still, she was surprised by the resilience of raw dairy cultures. Left to their own accord, milky products digested themselves by the autochthonous enzymes inherent in a raw batch of dairy, fresh from the goat barn; milk turned itself into clabbered cheese on the counter, cultured by its own juices, with predisposed leanings toward eternal perpetuity... until all the sugars were digested. Then the edibles phase of dairy science ended, and the souring agent's dance towards putrification began. Pasteurized milk, as a counterpoint, went off in radically different ways, often forming molds and was susceptible to all kinds of external contamination in the absence of its own endemic bacterial population. Willow had noted these differences over the years whenever she had dried up the goats for kidding time and had to buy milk at the store. Not all milks were created equal when it came to enzymatic caliber and threshold for fermentation.

Today, Willow had saved up enough milk from the goat's production from the week to make a batch of cheese. She emptied the combined milks into a large pot and began to stir the mixture on her stovetop, bringing it up to a warmer temperature. She stirred slowly, ensuring that her added cultures and coagulant were distributed throughout the cooking pot. She removed her spoon, blew a kiss to the cultures at work, and put the lid on her mixture. She turned off the heat and resumed staring out into the distance from her kitchen window. The sun had come out, shining rays of fierce warmth on the gorgeous but parched landscape once more.

Midday

From the peak of the summer and into the fall, Spruce and Willow Wilder spent the heat of the day laying low. Their siesta sessions took many forms, all of them predicated on the mission to stay cool under the oppressive California sunshine. While the sun grew their plants, it wilted them thoroughly. When they had been younger they found themselves out in the heat exploring hiking trails on the land and forging straight on through the blistering, sweltering, ridge top summer sizzle. Unlike their pot plants, they never were able to capture the photosynthesis principle. They no longer preferred such solar boldness for productivity's sake, and they scheduled their work lives as much as possible around the sustaining coolness provided by the mornings and evenings.

At midday, the Wilders convened in the living room for a long lunch followed by their book banter session. Full from a delicious repast from their gardens, they luxuriated in the den reading passages from their respective books silently until one of them found something that needed to be shared with the other. Sometimes the discussions about the readings occupied more of their time than the actual literature repose. They mixed equal parts of nonfiction and fiction, featuring articles, stories, academic fare, or popular writings. The recipe for their book banter, like their noontime, was loose and depended on many variables such as current events, everyday concerns, and curiosities.

An optional side of pot often added flavor to their sessions. Unlike their breakfast, which had used the baby greens of the cannabis plant chock full of nutrients but not yet in the exhilarating flower stages of the plant, their after-lunch musings were regularly punctuated by the decidedly psychotropic dried flower forms from their garden. Cannabis came in many forms. Dutifully utilitarian for fuel, fiber, and food, the plant could also be used for magical merry-mak-ing medicine (and often was on the ridge top homestead). Depending on which part of the plant the Wilders used, what the plant had been cultivated for, and which part of the growth cycle they had harvested the plant in, cannabis willingly served as a very versatile mistress for them. Willow sometimes served a sweet spoonful of canna-choco-late-butter to get them high; sometimes they would add a few drops of cannabis tincture to a cocktail or mocktail as the vector for their herbal dosing. Today, Willow rolled up a fatty with "White Widow," a favorite strain of the plant that had been cultivated last year to get them high, and they sat outside on their porch to enjoy it.

His and hers Adirondack chairs faced out to the lofty views of the hills rolling to the valley below them; wedged between them rested a small table Spruce had built from twisted madrone branches he found on the property. An old wine barrel top which Spruce had been given from a local winery friend served as the tabletop. Atop the wooden art piece sat an abalone shell ashtray for collecting the droppings from their joint as they passed it back and forth. They had spent close to thirty years performing this same ritual, exchanging a tent for a cabin, their freedom as a couple for a family with two children; and yet nearly every day they managed to exact this pre-scription to the fullest extent. Breathing in the burning flowers they had grown calmed them, eased their nerves, and made them smile time and time again.

Returning to their den, they both set to work on their cur-rent reading for their book banter. It wasn't long before Spruce was waving his copy of a book on historic California through the air, exclaiming, "This is it, Willow!"

Willow had been reading from a magazine and let the pages fall open on her lap. "Yes?" she inquired, smiling, bemused by his urgency; she was accustomed to his outbursts during their book banter, and for months he had been specializing in nonfiction accounts of California before the arrival of the settlers. He was on the search for something that would feel like a solution to any of the large problems that posed him regularly as a homesteader.

"It wasn't that California was a pristine ecosystem that was destroyed by settlers… although the argument that the land grab from the Native Americans destroyed California can be made easily enough. And I think it should be made more. But I digress. What this book is saying is that California was being cared for and stewarded expertly by the peoples that lived here before settlement. California's resources were keenly favored by the way the native people lived with the land."

Willow smiled, her right eyebrow raised inquisitively. "Go on. I'm with you so far."

Spruce caught his stride, "California's resources were abundant precisely because they were being tended by the Native Americans. It turns conservation discussions on their head! Instead of leaving the wilderness wild and untended, they are saying that the way that California was stewarded for thousands of years involved diligent application of human involvement to shepherd the forests, the streams, and the grasslands."

Willow agreed, nodding, "Yes, of course. People cared for the land and the land cared for the people. They were mutually beneficial."

"Right!" Spruce was standing now, the book fallen to his chair, and he was pacing as he spoke. "So, here we are on the homestead, doing what we can to steward the land in a way that is as responsible as our knowledge limits allow at present. The question is, can we do this and be settled? Can we tend the wild as modern humans? Can we coexist with California's nature in a way that benefits her as much as it does us?"

"So, California's a lady, eh?" Willow coyly raised both eyebrows this time. "I certainly want her to be cared for in the best way possible. She's taken good care of me all these years!"

"She's not just a lady, she's a goddess, a deity that combines the elements into balance," Spruce proffered.

"The book says that?" Willow asked.

"Not in the passage I was just reading… I think that's the pot speaking through my own tangential digression," he admitted. "She's our goddess, Willow!"

"Then, I hope we're honoring her properly." Willow started to open up her own magazine again.

"That's it!" Spruce enthusiastically grabbed her and brought her up to her feet, her magazine dangling from her right hand. "We need to honor her! This year, I want us to have a ceremony for her at the beginning of the harvest. Something that reaches to the sacredness of her contributions to our lives these past thirty years on this land. I want to thank her for this part of the land of California, this place that we have been calling home." He hugged Willow close to him and breathed her in.

"I like that. Perhaps we can make a ritual to include giving thanks to the land that birthed the plants when the trimmers get here." Willow smiled. "Blessed be our California gardens!"

The Wilders both struggled with a sense that agriculture, though satisfying to the soul and delectable to the palate, might have been a wrong turn in human evolution. They both questioned if staying in the same place in permanent structures was legitimate or not for humans. With permanence, in many accounts of peoples the world over, came disease and the ever problematic qualification of who has access to land, resources, and the "right" to practice their permanence. They both felt relieved to hear that tending the land, however problematic in the modern matrix, had precedent in Californian history in the era before settlement by colonizers. Both Willow and Spruce knew that they had found a way to thrive in California's landscapes as farmers, cultivating the earth where they had landed. And the incipient agenda to celebrate the land this year in a new way bound them to something bigger than their small narrative: it made them sacred witnesses in concert with the mysterious beauty of the land they had been cultivating throughout their adult lives.

Willow let the embrace hold. Tickled that Spruce had been so moved by his findings on land-based connectivity that he had attributed divinity to their Californian plot of land, Willow surrendered her body weight into her husband's arms. As she nuzzled into his neck, she envisioned the body of California as though its hills were breasts and hips undulating along the ridges. As her imagination exploded into a flurry of sultry landscapes, Willow let her own form press against her lover's. Spruce smelled Willow's sweet, earthy aroma and luxuriated in her presence, his own Goddess Incarnate. They both felt oddly uplifted by the suggestion of spiritual embodiment on their land and the creation of a ritual to honor the significance of land-based livelihoods. Aroused even, they started to sway back and forth in each others' arms, elevated by something to celebrate, an ecosexual win for them and the ridge top. Willow finally dropped her magazine, both arms needing to wrap around Spruce. Slowly, intuitively, they retired together to the bedroom for the rest of their "siesta" time.

Night

That evening, Willow took out her cheesecloth and poured the cheese curds and whey through the cloth. She let the bundle of curds which were caught in the cloth strain out the extra whey. She collected the whey into a bucket to give to the chickens, and she set aside a full half gallon jar for her own uses in the kitchen. Next, Willow got out a large mixing bowl. She chopped herbs she had gathered from her herb spiral on the side of her front porch and added salt and vibrant green flavors until she was satisfied. Carefully, she packed the herbed goat cheese into small pint glass jars, pressing the concoction down until a horizontal cheese layer formed at the top; to this she added a fine layer of olive oil to seal the batch. Finally, she screwed the lids on the jars, brought the jars to the refrigerator for storage, and grabbed some milk to heat up on the stove top.

Willow and Spruce went out together to the garden patch hand in hand with mugs of hot chocolate carried in each of their free hands. As the sun set on the Western horizon, the couple walked to the arbor way that marked the entrance to their Ganga garden. Each day they visited the garden was a day given in devotion to the beauty and mystery of life's unfolding dance. There were always surprises and adventures to be had in the garden. They sipped their desserts as they individually made their way around the garden, checking on each of the plants.

"They're looking great, Spruce," Willow said as she eyed a particularly rich plant, flowering in dense crystals all around a heavy, dense cola.

The plant she was speaking about stood higher than her and its branches had been trained in espalier fashion to grow out on the sides such that the result was a truly massive creation of marijuana glory. Their garden featured about ten different strains at the height of summer. About half of the crop had already been harvested and was hanging to dry in a nearby outbuilding. Twenty-five plants remained, finishing up their growth cycles in the garden. Those numbers were relatively modest in the rural Mendocino County industry. Bygone eras of legislative powers had deemed that one could grow twenty-five plants for medicinal uses under County decree. Some people grew for several patients and thus fulfilled a somewhat delicate legal agreement by posting the prescriptions for their patient(s) at the entrance to their gardens, theoretically allowing planting in multiples of twenty-five for each patient they covered. The question always loomed: under whose jurisdiction? Mendocino County had little enforcement as a singular entity busting pot farms, as the people had spoken and voted to have medicinal use legitimized in the early 2000s. However, the County would sometimes join larger drug task forces to combat the (very much still illegal at the national level) marijuana farms by bringing in DEA (Drug Enforcement Administration) agents who felt federal jurisdiction overruled local ignorance of the threat of this Schedule 1 Narcotic.

"We have so much to thank this plant for," Spruce stood gazing at the garden as a whole, not focused on one particular plant in the garden but rather sizing up the weed garden holistically.

"She's been very good to us," Willow conceded.

"How often does one really love the work that they do?" Spruce asked. "I love growing pot."

"It's a shame if this really is the last year," Willow spoke to the elephant in the ganga patch.

Legalization meant the end of an era for many small farmers who had been utilizing their backyard gardens to subsidize their alternative realities for a very long time. They both had been avoiding the subject as much as possible because they both felt that the end of their careers as Mom and Pop pot farmers had finally arrived with this, the last crop they were planning to cultivate.

"I have loved growing pot," Spruce corrected.

And then they were both looking off into the distance again. Something about their ridge-top homestead lent itself to horizon reflections and the zooming out to the bigger picture when personal issues were too difficult to comprehend. They maintained a tenuous positivity about their futures. The Wilders knew big changes came with legalization, but what they didn't know was how they would affect them. That answer involved too many variables and uncertainties for them to commit to much more than precarious ambivalence. Nobody, not even the local and state legislators, really knew what was going to happen to the California pot industry.

"When it's all said and done, there just isn't anything else a farmer can grow in a season that can make them $2000 a pound," Spruce admitted.

"With the black market tanking and the price in such a state of flux, we'll be lucky if we can still get $2000 a pound this year," Willow acquiesced. "The price has been dropping for years, but we're at an all-time low. Most of our friends are still sitting on their crop from last year, ready to bring in this year's crop without the usual capital they have become accustomed to. Trimmers are gonna take a cut in their payroll too."

Spruce nodded. He knew all of this well enough. There didn't seem to be much to say really. "I suppose it was inevitable... that the profits would be too seductive for the government to allow people to continue to generate that kind of income under the table for too long. We had a great run. We are part of the last great stand of the Wild, Wild West, growing wild west weeds to turn over an impressive profit. The green rush is over. Now we stay tuned to see what comes next."

They both sighed. Spruce went back to looking at the plants, checking to make sure that everything was ready for harvest that week. Even though they had spent decades growing this particular plant, they were still intoxicated by her wiles. Every spring they got her in the ground, and every summer they worked hard to cultivate the best looking plants. Several months of tending, expertly developing the attributes they most desired had always paid off by the fall with a gorgeous crop of weed. While they credited this herb for financially sustaining their family, they also developed her cultivation to a devotional practice. Some growers just wanted the money. But lots of growers, the Wilders included, were really in love with the plant and wanted to show off the art and craft of weed stewardship.

"No hemis?" Willow asked breezing over a hearty plant.

Marijuana plants produced a gender dichotomy in their growth stages. Females grew up to have luscious, psychotropic crystalloid flowers, and males grew up to have balls. Most growers didn't want much if anything to do with male plants because they were responsible for the pollination of the females and that sexy tryst produced seedy weed which considerably lowered the value of the pot at market. Males, if kept at all, were placed in an isolation area where the gardeners could collect pollen to carefully create seeds for future years by expertly applying the pollen with a paintbrush to select plants at the proper (sexy plant) places and with proper (botanist savvy) timing; if done poorly, pollination took hold of the single ladies, and progenitor pandemonium would ensue. However, in the absence of male plants, a female in an overly femmed-out area had occasionally turned into a male; these nonbinary, gender fluid pot plants were referred to in the trade as hemaphrodites or 'hemis' for short.

"All girls, all the time," Spruce responded with a smile.

"My favorite kind of party!" Willow laughed. "No offense to you, sweet soul. It's just that these ladies really know how to have a good time: a heart open time, a free your mind kinda time, a laugh and grow and transcend all the parameters of the conditioned mind kinda time."

"None taken. They're my favorite girls too. It's a helluva crop this year; it's a great note to end on if the song must be played out." Spruce kept checking the ladies, nodding affirmations to the beauty and success of each plant as he went.

"She's from all over the world. She's been here since time began. Her manifestations are gloriously unique but all irie as can be. She's my shero, and she always has been." Willow tenderly stroked one leaf as she continued to pour over the plants in awe of the work that lay before them.

"She's not everyone's cup of tea, but she's a versatile mistress. Food, fiber, fuel, and fun. Hard to stack all those functions in one fine plant specimen, but she fits the bill and heretofore has also been particularly well suited to our fine California climate. I'm counting my blessings, and she's way at the top."

"Thanks for the perspective. It's easy to be immersed in life's dramas and projects and forget to appreciate the many blessings we have right in front of us," Willow said, her eyes gazing into nature's crystallization artistry. "The heat has taken it's nightly reprieve. Waxing moon coming up, breeze feels divine, wanna take a fly over the moon with me? A magic carpet ride perhaps?"

"Yes! Carpet ride for two leaving from the 'Top of the World' ranch right now!" Spruce rallied back as he sat down on the ground in the middle of the garden.

"Circumnavigating the starry cosmos with Sativa and Indica as our stewardesses," followed Willow, as she joined him sitting cross-legged between the plants.

"Leave our baggage behind. Fly free."

CHAPTER 2

Tuesday October 3, 2017

Morning

"It's time to rise and shine lovely lady," Spruce said as he walked into their bedroom. "Seize the cool morning and then we can spend the rest of the day chilling at the river."

Willow opened her eyes, watching Spruce fawning over her with a mug of tea in his hand, ready to pass the herbal refreshment her way when she got vertical. She brought herself upright and paused to take a sip of tea. "Nettles and roses. Thank you." Spruce nodded warmly and headed out to the garden to begin his morning chores.

Willow slowly made her way up to the yoga platform in the trees outside their house. Her limbs were ready to stretch and move and awaken to another day. She loved these late season outdoor yoga sessions; the weather was perfect, and she could practice while looking out over the beauty of Redwood Valley. The ridge provided a vantage point for the rolling hillsides down into the valley floor and back up along the opposite stretch of golden hills. She set her tea down at the edge of the platform and began a series of sun salutations just as the sun was beginning to peek over the edge of the ridge. Quiet dawn coolness opened into the warmth and brilliance of another day and the return of the sun's presence.

In a relationship spanning several decades, Willow and Spruce Wilder had found a way of tag teaming each other with regard to land projects. They both carried different chores and concerns about the land as a general rule. In times of need, either could substitute for the other and run the systems that the homestead necessitated. They sometimes made use of this redundancy if one member of the couple got sick or travelled off the farm. Usually, however, the division of labor helped them both offer themselves efficiently in service to the areas that needed care. As a couple with mutual plans established for the flourishing of the homestead, each member of the partnership ensured that certain parts of the holistic enterprise be maintained. With effective time management for the chores on the land, the couple pragmatically conserved their energies and were both able to provide free, spacious, and creative time for other disciplines.

Today, Spruce needed to check on the water tanks. In a land of drought, water usurped everything else on the farmstead. Too far off the beaten path to utilize the municipal water and power access of the area, the "Top of the World" ranch capitalized on alternative methods to support them. They had created and maintained sovereign utilities as part of the ranch's infrastructure. The couple tended to a spring on the property, a pond that they built, and various catchment tanks that stored the winter's water bounty long past the time when the rains stopped coming down in California. The spring had lured them to buy the property back in 1980. Water security eclipsed every other concern the couple had about the location of the land. Because they had found a property within their means that had good access to water, they decided to go for it even though the ridge top land was at the end of a long dirt road and was virtually undeveloped.

Willow was pregnant with their first child when they began to live on the land. They spent the first year living in a canvas tent, walking the property, watching the seasons come and go and getting ideas about how best to build. After seeing the way water moved over the landscape, they made their choices about where to install a pond. As the years went by, through trial and error, they discovered just how much water would be required for them to irrigate their crops through the dry California summer. As their business progressed, they reinvested their income back into the land, developing more water storage and bigger food gardens. During the past ten years, however, the tanks had barely held enough. Each summer Spruce found himself carefully measuring the water levels in their systems. This year, fall had come and there was still no rain in sight. They had the spring as a steady water source and the pond as a redundant water resource available on the land. They were, in fact, far more water solvent than most of their friends. They hadn't trucked in water when the drought got severe to continue growing their crops, which had been drought protocol for many backroads growers. Spruce didn't expect anything to be off with the tanks, but he made checking them a priority so that there wouldn't be any surprises. Water is life.

Willow finished up her yoga session, lying down in corpse pose and taking in all the hues of the gorgeous dawn above her in panoramic colorgasm. Closing her eyes, she let the liquid pastels of this fall day wash through her, caressing her through every fiber of her being. She relaxed into an exquisite puddle of calm which weighed down her limbs and offered to sink her deeper into the earth beneath her.

Before the couple had settled on the land, Willow had spent her young adulthood traveling in India, devoted to ashram life and yogic practices. After coming back to the U.S. and settling down with

Spruce, she still took time nearly every day to center herself before moving forward to tackle the onslaught of life.

Spruce noted the lowered levels of the tanks. He jotted down some quick calculations about how much more water was available. They weren't sure how many more days or weeks would pass before rain would come. Nothing was certain in the California climate anymore. There were patterns that they had noticed from living for so many years in the same place. Still, the only pattern that was reliable now was that things were getting hotter and by extension drier, and more water was needed to maintain the systems than ever before. As a backup, he could always pump more water into the tanks from the pond. The springs flowed with a steady daily output which was utilized directly for consumption by the couple, the animals, and of course the gardens.

Each tank could provide over a thousand gallons of water storage. At present, these tanks were hooked into the water systems of the house, barn, and gardens. Additionally, fire hoses were at the house, barn, and garden sites. Years of dry fall concerns had moved them to make a better fire prevention system, just in case. The house and systems were all off-grid, so there was no concern about power going out or pumps not working due to power outages. The solar array covered their needs admirably as long as the sun was shining. The rest of the year, when fire wasn't such a big concern, they had a small hydroelectric system from a seasonal creek that generated what they needed by flowing steadily in the colder, less sunny times. Still, Spruce wanted to talk with Willow and go over their emergency plans once more. If a fire came, it would surely take both of them to fight it, and even that might not be enough; every day they attempted to do something to mitigate fire danger.

Perhaps these measures were way past overdue, but life on the homestead tended to be an endless stream of relevant, valid, and necessary projects. Prioritizing the tasks consumed their energy, and to complete their lists would require vastly more manpower than they had and more energy than they could sustain; and so they settled on making the most dramatic needs take precedence. Willow and Spruce hoped that they might develop a flair for prophetic visioning about what was truly going to be needed for continued survival that neither of them truly possessed. They were after all humans of a retiring age, still attempting to spend their time divided among creative, economic, and pragmatic pursuits.

They had made the land and their livelihood work for them in a venture capital kind of way. When they needed funds for this rural adventure in homesteading, pot generated income consistently and profitably for financial solvency. Forging a community from a couple and their children meant that they couldn't possibly do all the things that were required of them. They chose their errands carefully and hoped for the best. And, to date, their journey had been smoothly paved with the steady backbone of Miss Mary Jane, our lady of cannabis. Their reality had been admirably reliable for decades of business success. Ever looming above them was the heavy hand of legality, both the persistent fear of being found out for their business and the growing fear that legalization would change their business dealings decisively once and for all.

Spruce felt complete with his water inspection for now and headed back to the kitchen to eat. He got there before Willow had returned from her yoga practice, and so he began to prepare an omelet for their breakfast. As he was cracking eggs into a bowl, Willow returned looking vibrant.

"Living the dream," Spruce commented, watching his partner make her way to the kitchen table.

Willow smiled and asked, "We really are the last vestiges of the wild west, aren't we? Where else can you produce an illegal crop for a tremendous profit and use that income to fund your dreams?"

"That's rhetorical, right?" Spruce began beating the eggs, adding salt and pepper.

"I suppose there's still money to be made in cocaine, heroin, acid, and all the other illicit substances the globe over," Willow admitted. "Well, I suppose that all those other drugs have a more complex system of processing, refining, and packaging. We're just drying some flowers that really like to grow around here."

"We're growing them really well, cutting off the less intoxicating parts, and sending out the highly intoxicating parts to the world. We've been producing minimally processed pot progeny so long. Imagine all the people we have gotten high," Spruce mused while heating up the egg pan.

"What will Northern California be like without pot money?" Willow queried, running her fingers through her morning mane.

"On the books, Mendocino county is one of the poorest counties in the state. But that doesn't include the under-the-table current of currencies that have been flowing at a steady rate. Without those monies in the watershed, we might see a lot more poverty," Spruce said as he poured the egg mixture into the heated pan.

"I wonder how long it will take for the legalization process to settle? It feels like there are so many changes, and the biggest change people are feeling now is that the price has gone way down. But maybe there are advantages to a legal pot industry?" Willow set the table with two plates and silverware.

"We shall see. Certainly, legality could bring some benefits for stoners," Spruce smirked.

"And medical patients might have easier access to their medicines," Willow chimed in, as she put the tea kettle on the stovetop.

"And perhaps the state legalization will lead to further states legalizing, and then the final step would be to have a federal legalization. Decriminalizing pot does make me feel pleased in theory." Spruce added veggies and herbs to the inside of the cooking omelet in the pan, sprinkling goat cheese curds amidst the greens.

"However, we are gonna have to figure out a new way to pay our bills," Willow said adding lemon balm, peppermint, and red clover to the tea pot on the counter.

"Yes, as lucrative and seductive as a farming career in the illicit substances industry seemed when we arrived in Mendocino County, I didn't really figure in the retirement and social security aspects of our futures," Spruce admitted, sealing the omelet to let the flavors meld together.

"No, I don't think job security was our reason for becoming pot farmers. Although we've had a good run of it, with fairly reliable success. We've had good yields and good profit for many, many years." Willow brought the teapot and two small teacups to the kitchen table.

"We had a very reliable income until the market became saturated." Spruce served up the omelet in two pieces, one for each plate on the table. "But who can blame people for saturating the market? You can't exactly grow corn and beans and tomatoes and hope to get rich."

"And so here we are, and the changes are happening, and it's time for breakfast," Willow concluded, sitting down at the table.

"Bon appetit."

"To morning reflections on the marijuana revolution," Willow said raising a tea cup for a toast.

After breakfast and animal chores, Willow's acorn harvesting partner, Tanya, came over for a visit. The two walked out to the rolling grasslands of the homestead to search for acorns under the land's oak trees.

"Shall we start with the Grandmother?" Willow asked Tanya.

"Yes, I would like to see Grandmother very much," Tanya replied, taking in the view from the ridge top.

The two friends walked toward the Grandmother Oak quietly while weaving across the hilly landscape. Moving steadily, Tanya and Willow made note of different native herb patches along the way. They had met in an herbalist training school studying medicinal plants and medicine making a dozen years ago; they had been carpool buddies during the nine-month herbal studies program, and they found each other's company both inspiring and valuable. They had been two of the older women in the class, respected for their experience as elders contributing their wisdom to the school group. Their friendship deepened after they graduated, expanding to include forays into wildcrafting with the knowledge that they had garnered, now applied in the field.

While Willow had been born in California and had lived most of her life on her Northern California homestead, Tanya's ancestors had always lived in Mendocino County. Tanya knew the land in her blood and bones, and Willow was an incredibly willing student, always ready to hear what Tanya had to share about Pomo culture, native land management practices, and the honoring of the oak trees. Likewise, Tanya found listening to Willow's storytelling to be a delightful way to pass the time, and they often exchanged tales on their herbalist walks around Redwood Valley.

When they got to the Grandmother Oak her branches were immense, her trunk a mountain of beautiful bark, her body beautified with lichen tendrils amidst firm, green leaves. Mosses crawled up her form, grasses fanned out away from her base in all directions, and acorns were freshly fallen from their lofty abode in the trees to land on the soft, waiting earth below. Tanya brought out a pouch of offerings for the Grandmother, and Willow followed suit. Both women laid down their gifts on the ground. Tanya began to sing a song, while Willow made a small nature mandala out of the materials on hand near one of the oak tree's particularly impressive roots.

Together, they asked permission to harvest these acorns to feed their people, again giving thanks to the bounty of the Oaks. Willow and Tanya both had fashioned their own backpacks from wood at a workshop held by a local woodworker. They began to fill these baskets with the acorns. And so they continued along to other oaks, leaving gifts, asking permission, collecting the nourishing seeds, and giving thanks. When their baskets were both nearly full, the women burnt a small portion of mugwort as a smudge, saying a simple blessing: "May the oaks of this land prosper."

As they walked back to Willow's house, heavy loads in tow, Willow asked Tanya, "How do you think the oaks will fare if a fire comes to this land?"

Tanya lifted up an inquisitive eye, "It depends."

Willow urged her to continue, "On the size of the fire?"

"Yes, the size. The location. How much the land has been tended before the fire comes. How much fuel there is for the fire. The winds for the day."

"Anything else?" Willow wondered aloud, even though Tanya's list had been comprehensive.

"Willow, my dear, it's not a matter of if there will be fires but when there will be fires. We are in California, and this state breathes fire ecology. To spread seed and maintain itself, the land has a marriage with the flame. The fires have been coming to California long before the settlers came here, and the fires will continue because California burns. When the people of my tribe tended these lands, we mitigated the fire dangers and damage to our homes by control-burning areas."

"You mean, you started fires?" Willow was surprised.

"Responsible fires, Willow. We started and stopped fires seasonally. We contained fires. We burned the places that needed to be burned and made our best efforts to do so because my people see fire and the land as dependent on each other. The oak woodlands know fire."

"Would your houses ever burn too?" Willow felt like a child suddenly exposed to college level material.

Tanya rose an eyebrow and replied as they continued walking, "My people were burning areas so that we could be safe from the naturally occurring wildfires. We weren't just lighting fires and seeing what happened. We were tending the wilderness we were a part of. Our houses were part of the land, the trees we visited and related to were a part of the land, and the animals that lived there were a part of the land. We acted in service to the land and did so with as much prudence and respect as possible. When you are truly part of a landscape on a wide scale, as the Native people of these lands were, your body is interrelated to the land so much that there isn't a distinction between the body of the land and you!"

Willow nodded, feeling her own connection with the land after several decades at the ridge top. How much deeper would her knowledge be if it had been part of her culture, passed down to her generation after generation?

"Willow, our people were living in houses made of willow, grasses, and reeds. Mostly our people lived near bodies of water, congregating at lakes, streams, and rivers where food was plentiful and the fishing was good. Our houses didn't burn during our control burns; we had control burns so that we weren't in danger of having things burn that we didn't want burned. And we burned to be in concert with the nature of the place. But even if we suspend the history and pretend for a minute that we did have houses burn down, the grass shelters we created would just go back to the earth as ash, food for the soil."

They were close to Willow's house now. Tanya turned to Willow and pointed, "But that structure. That is not supposed to burn, and the things in it are not supposed to burn, and if it does burn, it is going to a landfill somewhere because it's too toxic to deal with." She shook her head.

"Let's hope it never comes to that. I have too many plastic appliances that would melt into unspeakable goo," Willow admitted.

Tanya laughed out loud. Her contagious laughter grew, and soon Willow began to laugh too. Two crones cackled on the ridge top to ease the tension of the environmental disconnection they both were trying to overcome. The two friends put down their acorn packs and hugged, still softly giggling about the absurdity of the modern matrix.

"Oh Tanya, what are we going to do? We who are living experiments in the prevailing conundrum of so-called civilization? We want to be close to the land, but we have lost our connection to land-based living," Willow offered somewhat unabashedly, wiping a tear from her eye.

"We harvest acorns, tend the oaks, and pray very hard. That's all we can do," Tanya replied resolutely.

"Yes! Thank you for teaching me about tending to the oaks! I'm excited to fill my acorn granary with the seeds of this land." Tanya had taught Willow about the Native storage practices of acorns, and the two had shared many a crafting session building a small structure from materials on the land that would be used to hold acorns for Willow and her family. Tanya had modeled the construction design from her knowledge of Pomo granaries, but they both decided to make a smaller version for Willow's homestead while they practiced the skills needed to carry out a full-scale model in the future.

The women's prototype in granary architecture began with a framework of fir poles; without tending, many fir stands were so dense that the compressed trees couldn't grow to their potential. If a few trees were selectively removed, the canopy was able to let more light in so that the other firs could utilize all the space and nutrients needed to grow fully. Therefore, most projects on the land requiring wood started with Willow and Spruce going into the forest to thin the trees.

The firs provided the wooden frame for the granary infrastructure. In their first year on the land, the homesteading couple had transplanted both willows and cattails to the pond to invite native plant populations back to their home site; they harvested and prepared these materials with Tanya's instruction. Long sections of willow branches and cattail fronds dried in the sun before they were spliced into more workable pieces, cured for a year, and woven to make the granary walls. Finally, they lined the inner body of the granary with redwood tree foliage to thwart insects and fungus from claiming the acorns as their own.

Willow set up a tarp on the ground near the house. The women spread their haul out, enabling the sun to dry cure the acorns over the next several days. As they were distributing the acorns evenly, Willow mentioned, "I was reading an article somebody sent me recently about a town that kept burning over and over again. It was just set up in the wrong place, and so the fires kept coming to take the town down because of the way that the winds blowed, and the fire got vacuum sucked into the town or something to that effect. Anyway, the people that had lived there, knowing that this was going to happen, built these massive earthworks and restructured the lay of the land so that fire wouldn't be pulled toward their homes. Now fire goes around the town; they made a way for it to be funneled away from their structures."

"No more burning blenders?" Tanya joked, and both friends started laughing out loud again. The women's comic outbursts diffused some of the tension implicit in their dialogue, and their laughter softened the absurdity of their contemporary plight.

"That reminds me!" Willow interjected between giggles, "I need to leach a batch of acorns. Time to fire up the blender before the fires get here!"

Midday

"Lunches are packed. I've got towels, water bottles, and weed. You gals ready to roll out?" Spruce asked.

"Yes, just finished blending up the acorns. They're soaking now, so I can make a batch of bread for the crew that's coming later this week," Willow confirmed.

"Lucky crew!" Tanya said, nodding her approval. "I'm ready to head out. Spruce, I've got my grandchild coming over after lunch, and you know how much I adore that child." Spruce and Tanya hugged, saying, "Until the next time."

Willow embraced Tanya, "Yes, let's meet at your place next week and visit the oaks in your neck of the woods."

"It's a date!" Tanya said, heading back to her car.

"We'll follow you out," Spruce added, as they all walked toward their vehicles. Spruce and Willow waved as Tanya drove her car slowly down their dirt road. The couple got into their truck to head to a swim spot on the Russian River. As they bumped along the rocky road, they both quietly took in the landscape surrounding them. The drive, itself a kind of mini-vacation, allowed them to survey the countryside they knew so intimately, forested with oaks, firs, pines, madrones, manzanitas, and chaparral. They would notice the seasons with the changing of these perennial landmarks as they moved through growth transformations and life cycles. Today, Willow noticed some roadside weeds that had wilted flowers around the seed pods ready to spring if provoked by an animal or the wind. She put on her sunglasses as they came out of the forest and drove through the rolling oak meadows that their road bisected. Clear, crisp blue skies, heavy with strong sun rays beaming down, quickly heated up the truck and the Wilders.

When they got to the river, both of them promptly took off their clothes and waded into the water in their swimwear. There wasn't much water left at this time of year, but they were deeply fond of what remained running. After their refreshing dips with their whole bodies submerged in the rejuvenating waters, Spruce and Willow put on their river clothes — loose-fitting, cotton fibers to cover exposed shoulders topped with sun hats. They were planning to wait out the heat of the day right there, letting the sounds of the lapping river take them into midday reveries.

As they were settling into their spot, another couple came hiking down the trail to the shore looking hot, ready for the water to deliver them.

It took a minute, but Spruce realized who had just arrived. "Oh good, it's you guys. I brought the OG kush," Spruce announced.

"Excellent," said Pedro, their neighbor and friend. "I'm game after a quick dip."

"Hi Maria," Willow said, waving as she unpacked lunch onto their picnic blanket. "How's retired life?"

"First fall in 20 years I haven't been behind a desk peddling math problems to misfits," Maria said. "I miss the kids of course, though I don't miss the incessant nature of a teacher's occupation, even though I loved being a scientist to high schoolers."

"True that!" Pedro added from the river. "We're planning a trip to Mexico for the winter. Get out of town, see some family, tour the ruins of pyramids…."

"Not grade one paper the entire time!" Maria finished for him.

Pedro laughed. "It's nice to have my wife back. Now we get to party!"

"They work schoolteachers too hard these days, don't they?" Willow said to Maria, but Pedro answered, "They did! But now she's free! Ayayay!"

"I'm glad you get a chance to relax and enjoy each other," Spruce added, getting out the OG kush pot strain from his tin.

Every self-respecting stoner in Mendocino County had a paraphernalia compartment that they travelled with at all times. Sometimes it was a simple cloth bag, enough to hold a few rolled joints. Other times it was a pint mason jar, filled with weed, papers, lighters, and filter materials. Spruce had a silver tin about the size of a breath-mint container, plain except for a turquoise strip across the middle of the tin. He carried his stash with pre-rolled joints and a lighter for all weather conditions in his pants pocket when he went out and about. For decades, this tin had served as a fully sufficient to-go kit; however, in the last few years, he had also carried a small roll of hemp with him. He proceeded to kindle the end of the hemp twine with his lighter. He drew the joint to his lips, brought the lit twine to the tip of the joint, and inhaled.

He promptly exhaled, letting the smoke go from his satiated mouth. Wispy plumes of intoxicating smoke left trails as Spruce smiled towards Pedro, proffering the joint before him with an extended arm.

"Why the twine, man?" Pedro asked as he headed out of the water.

"It's so I don't have to huff the fumes from this lighter," Spruce explained.

"Sounds good," Pedro affirmed, drying off with his towel and sitting down next to Spruce. "Not long before the Social Security checks will disappear and the apocalypse is upon us. Best to smoke pot today and smoke pot tomorrow." Looking Spruce in the eyes, Pedro smiled. Taking the offering into his hand, he brought it up to his lips. Such was the custom of the land, to receive the smoke that was being passed around. Stoners were a sharing bunch, and this gesture had been repeated countless times in the circles they found themselves playing in. With strangers even, joints were the property of the commons, although today the company was familiar.

Pedro toked off the joint. "Those are some tasty herbs you're packin' Spruce." Pedro nodded approvingly.

Willow extended her hand to Pedro, who passed the joint to her. She held out the joint towards Maria, eyes watching to see if Maria wanted a taste of the doobie too. Maria hesitated but then said,

"Just a little drag, to try the flavor." She took the joint, puffed a hit, and agreed with her husband: "Very yummy guys! Nice work."

Maria passed the joint back to Willow, who took a toke herself and then reinitiated the rotation by handing the joint back to Spruce in a full circle marijuana communal event. The quartet fell quiet except for the sounds of their pronounced inhaling and exhaling. The river gurgled as the waters played across stones and flowed through the fairly shallow late season bed. A red-tailed hawk called overhead, screeing as its wings opened wide to kite across the sky above the river. Everyone looked up, listening to the animated landscape.

"Lunchtime?" Spruce broke the silence. "We have lots of food to share."

The collective of stoner swimmers felt into their bodies, and the munchies guided them all to the picnic blanket. Willow and Spruce brought out smoked salmon, goat cheese, sauerkraut, and crackers.

"Did you make all this food?" Maria asked aloud, impressed with the spread; she was well versed in the quality of food the home-steading couple had produced at potlucks in the past.

"We didn't smoke the salmon," Willow responded.

"But she did culture the cheese and ferment the kraut and bake the crackers," Spruce admitted. "Not much salmon to come by these days."

They all stared out at the river, sobered by the salmon counts from the department of Fish and Game. "I heard that the Native Americans who hold the salmon festival up North cancelled this year's event for lack of salmon," Pedro sighed. "How many more wild salmon are there?"

"Not enough around here anymore," Willow said. "I think most of the salmon in Northern California are born in a hatchery."

"I've been reading a book this week that explores through historical documents what a rich place pre-settlement California was. By the descriptions I've been reading, Cali was teeming with wildlife. There are accounts of rivers with salmon runs so thick that you could walk across the backs of the fish to cross the river," said Spruce.

They were all still staring out at the river, where not a single fish jumped, and salmon sightings were regarded as more exceptional than customary these days.

"We're experiencing the collapse of the Native salmon," Spruce continued. "Unfortunately, we've dammed too many waterways with industrial sized dams that block the salmon from swimming upstream. They can't spawn if they can't return to the watersheds where they were born."

"There's so many variables. Beavers make small dams that turn out to be perfect waterways for salmon to do their thing. But, because their pelts became popular during the fur trade for hats, we hunted them to near extinction for fashion in most of the California wetlands. Turns out beavers were a keystone species," Willow added.

"Not to mention drought, global warming, and the intrinsic problems with water temperatures warming as the water levels drop," Maria articulated. "Also, agriculture draws water from creeks, so Norcal vineyards and pot farmers are sapping the water that would still be left for the salmon." Then she added, "No offense to you guys."

"None taken. We use rainwater catchment and our pond as water storage. We have a developed spring on the property and employ other water-saving measures like drip irrigation and mulching," Spruce replied.

"There are, however, lots of farmers that are in the pot industry out there only to make money, and they have no problem perching on forest land, tapping the resources, and sucking the water," Willow commented.

"Most of them are not farmers by trade. They're not exactly sticking to one place to build up their soil with their own composts. They're pouring bogus fertilizers to make big plants which then cause run-off, polluting the streams and creeks and rivers," Pedro added.

"We studied some of the craziest algae blooms in my class last year," Maria chimed in. "No doubt these were due to extra potassium, nitrogen, and phosphorus being added to areas where water was stagnating due to drought."

"In the Ukiah elementary schools, do they still have the science program with classroom kids raising salmon fry in aquariums?" Spruce asked.

Maria nodded, "They did last year. Been doing it for decades. I guess they release them at the end of the program into the wilderness, but unless the salmon can be in supportive watersheds again, we might be witnessing their extinction anyway."

"Maybe there's something in your book about salmonid restoration?" Willow asked Spruce.

"The Native Californians absolutely had an intimate relationship with salmon," Spruce granted. "I'll have to keep reading and see if there's anything proactive in there that could be implemented in the Russian River watershed today. It used to be that you could walk across a river in California on the backs of all the salmon swimming there. Not anymore…"

"Isn't the Russian dammed though? And the Eel River, too?" Pedro asked.

"Yes, both. They're both used for agriculture and household use. The Russian River Coyote Valley Dam project went into effect during the 1950s, and they actually flooded the Pinoleville tribal lands to build the reservoir," Maria confessed. "California may be a bastion of liberal thought today, but the Native peoples were subjected to horrific racism and forced relocation. The concepts of "Westward Expansion" and "Manifest Destiny" always sounded to me like history was being told by white people trying to justify the blood on their hands. Native people were murdered in cold blood for existing in the place that someone else wanted to be, even though they'd always been here, and they were a part of the land. To me, that is the root of so many problems: we forgot how to be stewards of this land because settlers tried to erase the Native population and their ways to justify their own means."

Nobody spoke another word, but they all let Maria's speech percolate as they took a moment to fathom the very gritty history lesson that had just been articulated. Maria paused while everyone considered the plight of the Pinoleville tribe.

"You take the people who are tending the land from the land, and the land may be sickened as a result. We are here purposefully. We are here to make our contributions. We are here to love the land and in turn we take our nourishment, body and soul, from the land. I don't have your answers about how to bring back the salmon, but the people who know salmon might. Being indigenous comes with an inherited knowledge of how to be in right relationship with the Earth Mother as her humble, devoted, and beautiful children. Sometimes too much time has gone by, too much trauma has been delivered, and the traditions have faded to a dull remnant of what they once were. But sometimes, and it is my strong belief that this is the case here… sometimes, a seed lies dormant until just the right elements combine to present the opportunity for growth. If we want to stay in California amidst the drought, the water and fire crises, we are going to have to stop complaining about problems we have manufactured and start showing up in a drastically different way, starting with honoring the people who lived with the land sustainably before the settlers tried to kill them all off."

Night

"I'm still thinking about what Maria said," Spruce admitted as they sat down over dinner.

"Because you agree?" Willow wondered between bites of salad.

"Because anytime hope is dangled in front of my face, I am suddenly rabid for it," Spruce granted.

"It's a fine kettle of fish," Willow admitted.

"Or an empty kettle of fish," Spruce countered.

"There's other fish in the sea still," Willow rallied.

"Yes, but they're bioaccumulating mercury and toxins in their fatty tissues while they swim through plastic gyre wastelands," Spruce threw down.

They both sighed. Living in the modern matrix meant constantly negotiating idealistic attempts to live sustainably with a paradigm bent on consumption, pollution, and disregard for the precious finite resources of the earth.

"Maybe we should go into environmental protection for our next careers?" Willow offered.

"We absolutely should," Spruce conceded.

"Do you think there will still be an Environmental Protection Agency in the future, or did they already get rid of the EPA in this presidency? Are we gonna be able to find such jobs?" Willow wondered. "I mean, at the rate things are going...," she trailed off.

"That should be our central governing office," Spruce said while gesturing with his right fist hitting his flat left palm.

"I don't think people want to admit how bad it has gotten," Willow shrugged.

"I don't think people know because the changes, while drastic, are situated in a cultural turning away from the wilds," Spruce said.

"You mean people aren't paying attention?" Willow asked.

"I mean the environmental collapses are in people's blind spots still," Spruce said. "Although every year that seems to be changing. Climate change refugees don't argue about the impact of environmental degradation on their lifestyles."

While the Wilder's evening contained a fair amount of hyperbole, they weren't grasping at straws. While fires were impacting California, hurricanes, tsunamis, acid rain, and flooding were popping up all over the world in other places. Abnormal storms brewed in eerily colored skies too often, and unseasonable shifts were becoming more noticeable even to lay people who weren't watching the progression of climate change. However, for years in California drought had loomed as a harbinger of doom, hand in hand with late season fires and the steadily increasing temperatures. As of yet, nothing had really impacted the Wilders personally.

"Some people are paying attention without the drastic catastrophes crashing down on them," Willow hoped aloud, musing on the ways that they had started to shift their own behaviors and practices to protect their land from dangerous potentials.

"Yes, but all people need to be united around protecting the environment," Spruce said again, firm and clear that his position was the only position.

"Yes, but we're 'protecting' it from us, aren't we?" Willow asked while making fake quotation marks in the air as she voiced the word "protecting." She continued, "paradoxes are hard to deconstruct in the public sphere."

"I guess it depends how you define 'us' to answer your question," Spruce concluded.

"Yes. You are still thinking about what Maria said," Willow determined. She knew that they were perched on the precipice of a formidable conversation about the depressing reality of the modern world. They often circled around to this topic, trying to find a tangible way to convince the world of the dire need for changes. Specifically, the Wilders both believed that without action to sustainably rehabilitate sensitive ecological habitats, they were unlikely to live through the future without witnessing the apocalypse.

Spruce pretended to dangle an imaginary (hope) carrot in front of their faces while proffering, "The problem is the root of the solution."

Permaculture principles had motivated Spruce and Willow to delve into creative solutions for themselves on the land; they had both trained in this approach to land-based stewardship. The method inspired aspiring permaculturists to seek out the problematic elements on their plot of land. Acknowledging difficult perspectives and understanding the complexities of their situation, they then explored what possibilities could be achieved to bring about lasting change. Using careful design methods which considered as many variables as possible, thoughtful decisions could be realized. Primarily, the methodology analyzed the ways that a home farm design would utilize the best interrelated components for the greatest ecological efficiency; however, Spruce wanted to apply the same concept to more universal conflicts to help solve obstacles in the social and political spheres.

"We can look at this in a new way and effectively come to an answer if we recognize our own disconnected stumbling," Spruce continued.

"Yes, I agree with what she said. The Native populations certainly have the answers to the question of 'how to be a sustainable steward,'" Willow admitted.

"Not a lot of Native Americans in the EPA though…," Spruce yielded.

"No, this country wasn't exactly founded on listening to and enfranchising the voices of the peoples that have lived here," Willow confessed.

"That's a bad joke," Spruce stopped the verbal rally.

"Who is joking?" Willow glared for a second at Spruce. "I'm all for it. Do you think it's going to happen? In this country? With the people in power electing to give anything to the Native Americans?"

"What other options are there?" Spruce wondered aloud.

These debates were par for the course for this couple. They regularly liked to spar about potential solutions to the environmental impasse when they felt like their personal actions weren't enough.

"The Native Americans were the very last people to be franchised in this country. We have a country founded on excluding the very people who most understand the land because to acknowledge such entitlement would have made it inconceivably inconvenient for the conquering bodies. Make no mistake, the people that lived here were subjected to a long and unending genocide so that their resources, expertly tended since antiquity, could be seized and utilized for the profit of the conquering powers. First by the Spanish and then by the Mexicans and then by the Gold Rushers and the Wild Westers, and finally by the trans-national corporations and the governing bodies of the deep state —all of whom profited exceedingly well from the land grab. None of them have ever thought twice about giving Native Americans anything but some shitty reservation

land, mostly outside of their preferred and long held territories."
When Willow finally finished, she took a long, deep breath.

"Yes, but maybe they could make reparations now?" Spruce
sheepishly added, not even really believing the words were coming
out of his mouth.

"You know how I feel about this topic. You know what is
required. You know what it would take," Willow's voice seethed in
her deepest vocal register.

"I know that's not on the table. I know we're still hurtling full
tilt at an economic future of infinite growth, and the powers that
be are still denying that we live in a bubble with finite resources. I
know that we can't sustain this gravy train. And I know that it's not
enough for us to be at the ridge top doing our best without the rest of
the community, the nation, and the planet also making institutional
changes that would have the potential to reshape the paradigm. I
know," Spruce admitted, "But giving in feels suicidal."

"I know. It's a fine kettle of fish," Willow said.

"Eat. It's more than we can resolve over dinner by a long shot."
Spruce looked at the dinner plate before him and Willow followed
suit.

"Short of a complete overhaul of the patriarchy, maybe we can
dine while discussing the fire precautions we would like to implement for the land. You know, something proactive," Spruce said
while forking up some salad.

"I just grieve that we're not better prepared as a modern people
for this ancient problem. California has known fire for so long. How
did we let it get away from us for so many years so that now we have
a really pressing danger on our hands?"

"We aren't from this land. Not in the way that we need to be to understand the issues that this land faces. We're Californians giving homesteading a try, make no mistake," Spruce debated between bites.

"I believe that our hubris has prevented us from truly appreciating what uneducated buffoons we are when it comes to actually being a part of this landscape. We have allowed ourselves to think that we are superior…."As Willow tried to finish her sentence, Spruce, mouth full, stopped her in her tracks to shout, "WHAT?!"

"Listen, you!" Willow cut him off at the pass. "I'm not talking about you personally. I'm talking about the way that we as modern peoples are all victims of institutionalized racism, and how we have been conditioned to a cultureless predator totem in which we are complicit in the rape of the land and indigenous peoples and their knowledge for our own gains and values," Willow paused. "It's not you. It's the system that raised you."

Spruce swallowed. "Go on."

"Conquerers don't ask questions about how best to be in harmony with the people of a place. They take over and they profit off the exploitation of the people and the land they have taken over. That is why Native Americans in this country have not been involved in the dialogues about how to be part of a progressive nation. To include them would be to hear about the very real shadow side of this country. Are we ready to admit that appalling history in all of its continuing ramifications? Are we ready to grieve those choices? And, if so, are we ready to apologize deeply? Are we prepared to take ownership and ask for guidance from the people we have been oppressing? Because until we are, as far as I see it, we're fucked."

"We're not going to be able to work this out over dinner," Spruce said, resigned to the quagmire they were wading through.

"No, we're not. And it's going to take a lot more than just us. This is beyond the personal. Way beyond it."

"The thing is, desperate people start to seek out desperate choices. Maybe the climate chaos will awaken the government to the atrocities that have been committed and from that place of disaster in hand, they will be able to ask for help," Spruce offered optimism tempered with a healthy dose of pessimism.

"Yes, perhaps at the 11th hour they will realize that the clock needs to be turned back before we're out of time," Willow admitted, exasperated.

"When do you think you realized that we were going to hell in a handbasket?" Spruce asked, trying to bring the conversation back to the personal and something more tangible than systems revolutions.

"When we had children," Willow smirked.

Spruce scoffed but then added, "Please continue."

"I think that was when everything changed. Until then I wasn't as invested in the globe spinning on its axis. If we all died from a nuclear winter, I was somehow unattached enough to accept my own mortality. But after I gave birth I was invested in a way that I've never recovered from."

"It sounds like you knew it was bad before then, but childrearing really sent that message home?" Spruce asked, much more at home with the personal than the political.

"If I died, so what? When I was traipsing about India learning about gurus who transcended their physical forms I thought that it didn't really matter anymore what happened to me. I was just a bit of cosmic stardust exploring incarnation's playground. I was young and reckless, and personal enlightenment was infinitely more compelling than trying to make systemic changes to society. The world was a big hot mess, and I could accept that."

"But then there was Lily," Spruce said her name, and it struck the desired empathic chord.

"My maternal biology overrode my consciousness every time. I needed the world to change so that she could live in it, survive in it, thrive in it."

"And then there was Forest," Spruce continued.

"Yes. By the time Forest was born, there was no looking back. I was committed to a world I had been prenatally dead to. Motherhood resurrected me from apathy. Motherhood planted me in the world and on the land and gave me new vision," Willow's face softened as she spoke about her children.

"Yes," Spruce simply agreed.

After a moment of reverie, she took her fork to a fingerling potato on her plate and raised it to point across the table at Spruce. "What about you? When did you realize that the shit was hitting the fan?"

Spruce put down his fork and thought for a minute. "I guess I've always known that we were doomed as a civilization. Not speaking prophetically, I just knew that we would need to make drastic changes if we were to survive. I think I grew up with atomic fear. We entered the world with an environmental reflex that hinged on radical changes happening 'or else.' But truthfully, for me, it built and built to a crescendo in the 80s with our kids too. That seemed to be when the mainstream collective started to discuss the environment in a more aware way."

"Ok, but when did it really hit you personally? When did you realize that we were personally in danger of dying because of the societal choices being made?" Willow interrogated further, this time waving a sun gold cherry tomato in Spruce's direction.

After a moment's respite to clear his thoughts, Spruce articulated succinctly, "2005."

Willow was surprised. "Why?"

"Forest and Lily were home from school that summer, and we were swimming at the pond. We had just made the island together and were all sunbathing on it when we heard a loud cracking coming from the hilltop. We looked up and saw the mother oak at the ridge top come apart at her seams."

"Oh yes! Of course." Willow interrupted.

He thought back, remembering the moment when his enchantment broke. "It was the middle of a heat wave, and the summer had been breaking all records for the hottest temperatures ever achieved. We were all home together, and we were doing our best to stay cool. Watching the kids watch that tree... that tree that they had grown up with and hiked to and climbed on and celebrated their whole lives with ... break and uproot without any reason broke me. The climate change reality took on a new implication for me then, and I think that took my understanding to a new level because it became personal. I loved that tree. Our kids loved that tree. It didn't come down in a storm or logging incident; it came down because it couldn't survive our abuse anymore. The heat of global warming claimed that tree. It wasn't a theory anymore. It was ecological terrorism, and I realized I had been complicit or apathetic when it came to being involved in any activism to stop it. I had been waiting for the ball to drop, and when that oak toppled that was the peak moment for me. From then on, I started to research more consistently and study more ardently the ways that I could be more sustainable." Spruce finished.

"It moved you from the theoretical to the personal," Willow concluded. "Your story explains precisely why we will not get to the bottom of this issue over dinner. The somewhat invisible causes of environmental collapse are seen most dramatically from a retrospective illustration."

Spruce continued, "To inspire change from a regime in which the environment has been fractured into consumable parts to a holistic model that embraces an intimate reckoning with our earth as the most essential provider for our livelihood does require some kind of awakening."

"Oh that I will live to see the day when humanity issues a proclamation for the protection of the planet!" Willow exclaimed.

"Yes, that it may happen in time," Spruce softly added.

"In the infinite potentials of the outcomes of our existence, I see two eras of humankind." Willow numbered 1 with her right index finger. "First, our present era, in which we do not live in unity with the planet Earth and all that she entails."

"Ah yes, I'm familiar," Spruce nodded.

"And second, the era in which we realize my first point and take action."

"What if the second never comes to pass?" Spruce queried.

"Null and void. Seeing as we're currently having this conversation and we are both most palpably not excluded from existence, the second point is presumed as evident and relevant."

"Arguably so!" Spruce smiled. "So perhaps the qualification of your second point requires a clarification as to the quantity of 'we' you are referring to?"

"Clever point," Willow admitted. "Personally, I believe it will take more or less all of us."

"It's that big. That important," Spruce intoned.

"SO…." Willow was buying time as she thought through her next point. "So, we need to appeal to everybody. We want all hands on deck."

"Luckily, everyone who is alive and desires to maintain that condition gets to be included in the category of creative action to address this. There are many levels of the shift embedded in this, and it's going to take all of them. In all their infinite unfoldings," Spruce added.

"Not all of them. I'm happy to cut out any of the infinite possible outcomes that involve the continuation of the patriarchy. We can cull those immediately," Willow mused.

"And I'm happy to include all those solutions that involve restorative healing. It would be incredible to see the Native Americans get to school the state about healthy relationships to fire. It would be amazing to have the Native knowledge and culture that has been repressed and oppressed until now finally seen and acknowledged as wisdom carrying traditions. Old technologies could be appreciated as new technologies to resolve present-day conflicts," Spruce said in awe.

"Right! Yes! Absolutely!" Willow giggled. Spruce smiled. They both had agreed and celebrated by clearing their dishes from the table. Another meal enjoyed together.

Willow began to soap up a sponge. As she ran the first dish under the faucet, she turned to Spruce and said, "But how do you get people to do what's right? How do you convince people to make lasting change?"

Spruce walked up to the left of the sink carrying a cooking pot to add to the washing line-up.

Willow continued, "short of a spiritual rebirth in which everyone recognizes and internalizes the principles of environmental care implicit in proper Earth stewardship?"

"Money," Spruce interjected while reaching his hand to take the washed and rinsed plate from Willow with a dry towel. "Economic profit."

"Yes, that is the way of the current paradigm. So, how are we gonna show them the Benjamins?"

"Environmental Protection jobs in the Forest Service. Well regulated and scrupulously maintained environmental projects that harvest wood selectively and create value-added products from the wood," Spruce answered.

"So you pay people to log and then they go logging so that they can sell the wood?" Willow put down her washing and put her hands on her hips. "How is that better than what's currently happening?"

"Well, it's not exactly logging. There would have to be an understanding of the scale of the tree removal and a methodology that works to sustain the forest while making it more able to handle regularly controlled fire maintenance," Spruce suggested.

"Ah, so the spiritual rebirth piece IS implicit in your answer," Willow proposed.

"And the intentional starting of fires part. That's an addition. There would need to be people with the knowledge of how to contain control fires involved in the solution. To reduce extreme wild fires by producing small, regulated fires within ecological systems in the state's forests. Small, regular, maintained fires would be more responsible than the unmitigated super fire beasts that we have now whenever a fire starts at the wrong time and in the wrong place," Spruce recommended.

"Namely, summertime is the wrong time, and the areas that haven't been maintained through burning for too long are the wrong places," Willow reflected back. "Tanya and I were just discussing this. I like it, honey. That's very reasonable. I can see how the economic incentive will increase the chances that people will give a damn in our capitalist regime." Willow gave Spruce a hug.

"Speaking of money, I'm going to go harvest some plants to hang," Spruce said, heading out the door towards the garden.

As he opened the door, they heard the howling of a pack of coyotes in the distance. Their vocal improvisations were carried across the ridge top, signaling to the evening that they were up to their usual mischief; the moon shone her bright waxing light in gibbous form over the valley, encouraging her animal children to sing her lullabies.

CHAPTER 3

Wednesday October 4, 2017

Morning

Willow harvested fresh, "wet" CBD rich leaves for culinary projects from the kitchen garden using a large basket with a cotton towel draped along the insides of the weave to collect the goods; the CBD strains added nutrition but would not render her high. She set up her juicer and blender in the kitchen next so that she could make some juices and pestos to put by in the freezer. She lined up several clean jars to fill on the counter and began to mechanically macerate her product. As she was getting her green on, Spruce entered the kitchen.

"What if this wasn't our last season growing weed?" Spruce offered as he tidied up the dish rack.

"Good morning to you too, my dear," Willow said between pulses on the blender.

"We are really good at what we do. Just how much do we think that legalization is going to change the industry?" Spruce questioned for the first time. They had been skirting the issue for months, trying not to talk about it whenever possible. The variables were big and the terrain was thick, and there didn't seem to be a way to negotiate their careers through the changes they were seeing. "I have to ask. It's that personal piece again. We need to know where we're headed. We've got Forest and the trim crew coming later this week, and I guess I just want to know if this is going to be it or not. I want to talk through where we stand and what we see together so that we can make our decision."

"Have some juice," Willow said as she handed him a pint jar with cannabis and watermelon liquids marbled together in greens and pinks.

"Thank you," Spruce nodded and took a sip of juice. "Delicious."

They both smiled tentatively, looking into each other's eyes, hoping to keep the conversation civil. They had carefully avoided discussing their viewpoints at length, instead interjecting short commentaries on the developing playing field as the changes had trickled down to them over the past several years. Spruce still felt the inertia to cultivate herb from decades spent growing his annual marijuana patch on the land. He knew that whatever decision they made, they needed a mutual marijuana consensus to move forward and to plan for their future. They were life companions first and business partners second.

"I think that we should continue to grow our own plants for home use," Willow said. "With regard to the financial harvest.... Well, I just don't know. I can't see how it's going to be anything but our last crop."

Spruce sighed and sipped his drink. "What is our bottom line?"

Willow paused, wiping her hands on her kitchen apron. She turned to face Spruce. "I think that the bottom line is that the money is gone from the market, and unless you have a plan that will change that, we're just putting ourselves into risky business."

"But growing pot has always been risky business." Spruce countered.

"Growing pot in Mendocino County has always been a valuable source of income for us. It has allowed us to mostly work from home and afford a lifestyle that would otherwise have been difficult to manifest. We own land, we own our home on that land, and we are able to feed ourselves with consistently high-quality food. We've benefitted from the herb in every way that matters economically. And now the economic piece has shifted, and we can decide to move on to the next thing or we can continue to bank on something we have both confirmed is on its way out as a cash crop… at least in the ways we have known it to be profitable."

"I guess the current risk is that I won't be able to sell this year's crop for $2000," Spruce admitted.

"Seeing as last year's crop didn't go for that, I would say it's a good bet that this year's price per pound will be even lower," Willow added.

"The market's just glutted. Too many people are trying to capitalize on this last wave of the black-market pot industry," Spruce said, considering why they were up against the conclusion of their careers so abruptly.

"Absolutely. People have come from far and wide to make their riches off pot. But that wave has passed. Certainly, there are drug lords who have made big money off pot in the past couple of years, but largely what I think we're seeing is that the smaller businesses, ourselves included, are not going to be able to continue to sustain this livelihood beyond this fall. There are too many people in the game, too much product available, and the risks are getting more bureaucratic as permitting puts people on the books. I don't want to be written up in some office for being a pot grower. I don't trust that is going to pan out well. And besides, the funds to even get the permits in the first place… the additional costs are prohibitive for us to make another scene lucrative if we're selling the product for less and less." Willow scooped herbal pesto into a jar with a spatula as she delivered her speech.

"But Mom and Pop pot farmers like us have been doing this for decades. Surely there will be some acknowledgment that we know how to grow awesome weed, and we'll still be able to maintain a black-market value for the product," Spruce said hopefully.

"Our knowledge base is undeniable. The product speaks for itself. But in a market where people aren't paying attention to the quality of what is grown, do you really think you'll be able to make a profit that matches your investment of time and energy? Do you think that the college kids buying 1/8s are going to care if their weed was grown outdoors and organically?" Willow continued to fill jars with pesto as she spoke.

"Well, that's a point of discussion. Who will still want to buy outdoor organic?" Spruce chimed in.

"You know and I know that people like us are hoping that we can sustain a niche market. We're expecting that gourmet users will still want to be catered to with high quality weed products as legalization evolves and the dispensaries become saturated with available herbs," Willow acquiesced. "Just because we want that doesn't mean we can swing it. Where Forest used to be able to distribute to a dispensary, he is now going to need a legal permit to do that. We're going to have to get a permit for the garden if we want to sell at a dispensary. Are you really ready to make the leap from being a rural farmer who grows on his land to inviting the law enforcement to come and inspect the property to make sure all our i's are dotted and t's are crossed?"

"Maybe?" Spruce paused, considering just how dramatically different his occupation would be as a legal pot farmer. "I can't figure out if the cost is going to be too great. The permitting means that the government is now going to take a really big slice of the pie right up front. And then the dispensaries will take a chunk post-production. It's hard to estimate just what the cost will truly be," Spruce calculated.

"It's not only hard to calculate, it's guaranteed that not all pot farmers are going to make it. The small farmers here stand to lose. It's not a new pattern. Big money investments to grow weed for the masses are already lined up with large corporations. Big buy-outs and pay-offs are going down as we discuss this. Where there is money to be had, there will be large businesses ready to capitalize on it. The California agricultural belt is being targeted as a potential place for a new herbal mega-agro business takeover. Large-scale production can hardly wait for legalization to allow corporate interests to make whatever money is left to be made by a legal marijuana industry. That part is truly unfortunate. I'd hate to see Big Tobacco in particular profit from this plant," Willow admitted.

"Changing it from a small crop with a small profit dispersed amidst a large population of Northern California residents to a centralized large profit that is distributed by the few that own the agricultural conglomerate businesses does worry me," Spruce admitted.

"So, the real question I want to ask you is why you think it's worth it?" Willow asked. "Honestly, I feel like the writing is on the wall. The Wild West is gone, and the profit that pot was able to generate during the last 30 years was something special. We were some of the last free peoples able to earn a living with small-scale agriculture, and I give thanks that we used that money to create some security for ourselves. We have a home, we raised our children on the land, and now we have to figure out our retirement. I don't think that I would enjoy being a pot farmer under the new laws, and I don't think that our dreams are possible with pot anymore."

"It might be possible to make a profit under the table still. After this glut clears out, the market might balance out again and black market weed could retain another reasonable profit," Spruce ventured.

"Economic speculation does not pay the bills. And, if we get fined, we cannot pay off our court fees in weed."

"Yeah, I know," Spruce determined, head down. "It's the last harvest for us. Sometimes you have to get uncomfortable to face making big changes."

"I think that what we are experiencing is a bit of grace. We can leave now and be at peace with our contributions, knowing that we had a great run," Willow came over to Spruce to massage his shoulders.

"It's probably for the best. There's a lot of gossip going on about what's going to happen. Some people who have gone for the permitting this year are concerned about facing fines for back taxes, for the crops that they didn't ever record," Spruce commented.

"What?! How could they pay taxes on a narcotic? Isn't there the fifth amendment?" Willow was confused.

"Well, a few families I know have gone for the legal route with the promise of 'amnesty' for them. However, it looks like they might to have to deal with the IRS even though their income was decidedly not legal in the past. I guess money is money and they want their taxes paid, and the government is going to see what they can wring out of the people who have not been paying taxes on their incomes all these years," Spruce capitulated.

"Clever sharks they are!" Willow snorted.

"That's not all. I hear that up in Humboldt County they are starting to crack down on Mom and Pop farmers by delivering paperwork saying that if these pot growers are not in compliance with the law and if they do not get permitted (i.e., cough up thousands of dollars to be on the books), then they will be fined something like $15,000 per day until they are in compliance," Spruce offered. "If we can't grow the weed to pay the bills, they have us in a vice."

"Yes, I was discussing this with Forest's friend Jack the other day, and he said that there were going to be violations for lack of permits but also water rights violations if people were using water in the backwoods that they didn't have legal access to. They're coming down hard and using as many means as possible to funnel people into having to buy into legal compliance," Willow admitted.

"There's always the chance that we could stay under the radar. I mean, isn't that what we've been doing for decades?" Spruce asked.

"Yes, we have. But they just upped their game. Right now, for me, it feels riskier than ever."

"Because they're paying attention now?" Spruce asked.

"Because I'm paying attention now! I'm seeing the changes with my eyes open," Willow said collecting the jars of pesto to bring to the fridge. She carefully stacked them into the cool storage and turned to Spruce. "If you really want to know what I think, I believe that we should finish up this season, and we should retire from this career. We can stay tuned to see what goes on for our neighbors and friends and how this plays out for a few years. If the black market comes back up, if the permits are really as exorbitant as they seem, if the law enforcement is as thorough as it seems to be becoming…. We pay attention to how this shakes down. And then we make a more informed decision based on what we see playing out."

"Ever the practical drug lord my dear," Spruce joked.

Just then a chicken wandered in through the open door. Willow sat down on a chair at the kitchen table and the chicken executed an awkward head bobbing, feet prancing maneuver towards Willow. She picked up the hen and began stroking its feathers on her lap. The bird, accustomed to such niceties, relaxed, tilted an inquiring eye, and made soft exclamations as Willow said to Spruce, "I just hope we make it through the season."

Willow scooped up the chicken, carrying it back to the outdoor pen. While their chickens were mostly confined to the barn, they had a few bantam chickens that flew over their fencing enclosures. Depositing "Chickweed" back in the chicken run, Willow headed across the homestead to the garden to tend to the compost. Spruce and Willow had spent a day earlier in the week mucking goat poop from the barn. They had layered the poop with some vegetable cover crops they had grown to fill out their piles. Large tarps waited on the sidelines to cover the piles when the rains arrived. Until then, the piles had a light covering with straw. Willow extracted a thermometer from one pile, checking that the temperature had started to get good and hot. Heated by the activity of fungus, bacteria, and insects that broke everything down, their pile of poop metamorphosed into a nutrient-dense compost. Giving thanks for the alchemy of bugs, Willow imagined spreading the compost onto her garden beds next spring; she loved to foster growth from what had been waste.

Midday

"I'm headed down the hill to meet up with Susan for lunch. Need anything from town?" Willow asked as she plucked up her purse and gave Spruce a kiss on the cheek.

"Just more foodstuffs for 'Camp Trimmer' would be good," Spruce responded, smiling.

"On it! See you later, love. Give Forest a squeeze for me," Willow said, walking out the door.

As Willow walked out to her truck, her son drove up in his. He hopped out and gave his mom a big hug.

"Can you convince your father that this is the last year we're going to grow?" Willow smiled as she looked into her son's eyes.

"I'm done," Forest said simply.

"That's my boy," Willow said, smiling. "See you for dinner tonight? We can discuss the harvest scene together."

"Yes. I'm all ready for the grand finale of the ridge top pot," Forest smiled.

Spruce came out to the door to greet his son in jest, "Did she give you a disclaimer about my conflicted feelings for continuing our pot growing career?"

"More or less," Forest said as he embraced his dad.

"I'd like to think that we were all in a consensus about this. If we're going to stop, I want us to at least all be on the same page about ending this business as a family," Spruce intoned.

"Well, we've reached the era of legalization, and that does have new threats, new consequences, and new economic problems for our family business," Forest admitted.

"Let's walk around the garden while we talk. We can pick up some veggies to make lunch, too," Spruce suggested.

Forest smiled and picked up a basket from the front porch, "you lead the way, pops."

Spruce opened the gate to the pot gardens first, "The girls are mostly harvested and hanging, but there are a few left as you can see. We've got half drying and half getting their last days of sunshine," Spruce said as he gestured to the remaining plants, resplendent in their glory, grown outdoors in the summer sun of California.

"At least we get to go out with a bang! They're beautiful, dad," Forest said, smiling as he looked over one plant. Smelling the flowering cola, he gently closed his eyes, feeling ecstatic to be back in the herb garden.

"So, you feel like it's the end then?" Spruce asked his son.

"I think we both know that it's been coming down to this season for a few years now. There's not much to be done at this point. You could conceivably join the permitted legal world, but the profit margins will be reduced considerably, and that avenue is not without its risks too. I think it would be a good time for you and mom to retire," Forest suggested.

"Well, if you're out, then that makes it easier for us to get out, too," Spruce concluded.

"I'm out. I'm not a big business or any of the other corporations who stand to profit from this agribusiness changing from illicit to government-sanctioned legitimate," Forest said. "Who knows what will happen to the strains in the hands of the corporations?"

"Yeah, I don't want to be in the trade anymore if genetically modified pot comes on the market," Spruce granted.

"Well, I don't think that will happen right away in Mendocino County. We've banned GMOs and so, for now, that's holding court," Forest digressed. "But what really remains to be seen is what is going to happen with legalization in the larger courts. Even if the entire West Coast legalizes weed at the state level, will the feds view that as outside the purview of their jurisdiction? Because if not, then big businesses aren't likely to take that kind of hit. I think that enough states have legalized now that the question is more clearly: when is the U.S. going to legalize marijuana?"

"And if they do make federal weed a reality, what exactly is the benefit of that? Besides being able to grow, carry, and smoke weed on bigger road trips?" Spruce laughed. "Come on, let's go over to the food garden."

As the father and son walked through the garden picking out things for lunch, Spruce said, "I'm glad that we got to be on this land all these years. I'm not sure how we could have financed it without pot, and I'm eternally grateful that you got to grow up with country sensibilities."

Forest chuckled. "When you say 'country sensibilities' do you mean managing a weed farm or just the black-market distribution part? Either way, I think that this is my cultural heritage as a Nor Cal kid."

"Maybe not the best preparation for the rest of the world now that the market is tanking, huh?" Spruce wondered aloud.

"Shrewd business is shrewd business whatever the product," Forest chided. "Besides, I'm certain that getting to grow up on the land with fresh water and clean air were inheritance enough. You did a good thing getting this property back in the day. So many kids in the city don't have any dirt to relate to. I'm grateful I know how to grow my food and my medicine too."

"So, if we stop growing up here, what will you do? Oakland's got a lot going on, I suppose," Spruce asked while picking a ripe heirloom tomato off the vine.

"Well, Marcus and I have been talking pretty seriously about adopting…" Forest confessed.

Spruce was about to pluck a cucumber when he registered what his son had just shared. "That's fantastic news!"

"I mean, we could have had kids as drug dealers too, but it feels like it's time to start a family, and getting out of the industry just seems like it will make the process smoother," Forest confided while harvesting a long, purple eggplant. "I think that we have enough hoops to jump through as gay dads."

"You're going to make such a great dad!" Spruce gushed excitedly, putting his arm around Forest and leading him back into the house to prepare lunch.

Willow parked her truck a few streets parallel to downtown where unmetered parking was abundant. She walked for a few minutes to her lunch meet-up spot so that she could have several hours of peace before she would need to move her vehicle again. As she was strolling down the boulevard, she noticed that more shopfronts were empty than ever before in her memory.

"Willow!" Susan shouted, waving as she approached her.

Willow was in a daze as she looked at the storefronts. "They closed the used book store and the organic clothing place."

Susan swept Willow up in a hug, but Willow was limp at best. "I know, it's worse every time I come downtown too. Seems like another business has gone under with every town errand I run," Susan said staring at the empty building with her friend.

"Has online shopping really tanked our small town economy once and for all? Are big box stores all we're going to have left?" Willow asked, deflated.

"Well, corporate conglomerates are absolutely behind this, but I think that the end of the pot heyday also means that under the table money can't subsidize people's small businesses anymore. I think what we're seeing is the end of small business in America, whether that business be book selling or getting people high on weed," Susan shrugged. "They haven't closed the sushi restaurant yet. Wanna grab a bite?"

Willow and Susan walked arm and arm to the restaurant. As they sat across from each other, they chatted while they breezed over the menu.

"Downtowns are supposed to be the most prosperous part of a town," Willow said as they fingered the menus.

"Real estate in California continues to rise. I know it's high everywhere, but it's ridiculous here. I don't think places can afford to stay in business downtown," Susan added. The friends hadn't seen each other in over a month, and yet they hit the ground running, immediately venting their frustrations of the day.

"On the books, Mendocino County is one of the poorest places to live in California. But we both know that pot money has been subsidizing everyone. It's easy to spend money when everybody has a bit extra coming in from growing or trimming. What's going to happen when those jobs aren't available anymore?" Willow asked as the waiter walked up.

"We'll start with two miso soups," Susan ordered. Then, as the waiter headed to get the starters, she continued, "Well, it's going to be more than the storefronts that are forced to close."

"I mean, the more the cost of pot goes down, the more down-town is in decline," Willow argued, still thinking about the for sale sign on the used bookstore window. "I still had credit at that bookstore!"

"It's gonna hit everybody pretty hard. We might be in a bub-ble on this one, but I feel like everybody I know grows, trims, or sells pot," Susan admitted, completely aware that they were in a public place openly discussing the industry. Such was the custom of Northern California, and how pot, for most people was an extension of the culture and an accepted part of life.

"Well, I think this is our last hurrah," Willow said, looking over the sushi menu more closely.

"Us too. We have everything hanging already. We are hoping to offload it all in another month and then go traveling while we adjust to the new post-pot idiom," Susan responded, also scanning the menu while talking. "The 'irie roll'… does that have cannabis in it?"

"I don't think so. CBDs are on the market now, but I don't think they've made the leap to restaurant certification quite yet. But I could be wrong. This is Mendocino County," Willow said with a mischievous twinkle in her eyes.

"That was delicious, dad. Having homegrown food really makes it worth the drive to come home for visits!" Forest said, patting his belly, satiated.

"Time for some herb?" Spruce asked his son, bringing out his psychotropic play bag.

"How about something with your pineapple blend for dessert?" Forest suggested.

"That's gonna take a trip to the vaults," Spruce said, standing up, ready to retrieve the desired strain.

Father and son walked to the back door nearest the kitchen where a larder had been dug into the ground. Spruce opened the larder door, and both climbed the stairs down to the family's cool storage zone. The area occupied roughly the same dimensions as the kitchen below the main level of the house. Slowly, the two picked past the aisles of potatoes, squash, corn, and bushels of garden food that the family had put by for the winter, dimly lit by the overhead bulb. They came to the depths of the root cellar where a wooden cabinet Spruce had custom built by hand occupied the bulk of the far wall from floor to ceiling. Spruce slid open the cabinet door, and it revealed quart and gallon jars of all the weed they had left from the past season. Spruce procured a glass jar two thirds full with a light green specimen. He opened the lid and passed the jar to Forest. "How's that smell?"

Forest took a whiff and pulled out a large bud from the jar, holding it up in front of him. "Let's smoke this one."

Spruce picked up a two-foot length of garlic with dried flowers woven into the braid, "Take this back for Marcus from us."

"He always appreciates your culinary indulgences. And I enjoy the rewards of your generosity too whenever Marcus cooks. Since he finished culinary school, he's been looking for possible restaurant locations around the city. We've thought about buying a food truck too," Forest shared.

"Maybe we could grow the food for your truck... or for a restaurant in the bay. Farm to Table is all the rage these days," Spruce offered.

"I'll mention that to Marcus!" Forest said, slapping his dad on the back and stepping up to take the garlic braid.

"Mmmm. My sushi has that umami thing going on," Susan said between chopstick mouthfuls.

Willow picked up some pickled ginger and gesticulated with it while she said, "Maybe I should open a restaurant." Susan, mouth filled with sushi, dropped her jaw. Willow laughed at Susan's expression. "You have a better retirement package in mind?"

Having finished chewing her roll, Susan interjected, "You guys don't have any retirement plan?"

"Well, besides what we have buried in the ground, which won't last us until death, I'd say no. I need some supplemental income. I'm a crone, and I need a new job," Willow admitted poking at an errant edamame bean with the end of her chopsticks.

"You are an excellent chef, but running a restaurant is a demanding field to start in your golden years," Susan debated, shoving another roll into her mouth.

Willow nodded and excused herself to go to the bathroom. She closed the door behind her, locked it, and sighed as she went before the sink and looked up at herself in the mirror. She watched with interest the places where her face had become contoured with wisdom streaks. She studied the lines that gave way to creased terraces on her complexion, folding from her forehead towards her nose as she stretched and moved her facial muscles. Not unlike her hilltop garden, the materials of her face had undulating movements that had evolved with time. She stretched her skin up and down and around, seeing the textures perform unique movements as she furrowed her brow or stretched her mouth open wide. While she had to admit that the landscape of her face had added more rows and lines, her countenance remained peaceful owing to a cultivated aesthetic of health and earth-based living that ripened as she matured. Accepting the geographic nuances of her aging visage, Willow inhaled deeply, splashed her face with water, and witnessed gravity's momentum as the droplets flowed along her cheeks and down her chin.

She returned to her table with Susan, sitting down refreshed. "Sometimes I feel like I could retire now, and other days I feel like I am in my prime, ready to achieve the next great adventure. I feel passionate about what I do. I've spent my whole life getting clear on who I am and what I bring to the table. I know so much more than ever before," Willow said as she felt her low back aching that dull but consistent throb that came on at the end of the busy summer season. "But my energy does feel like it's changing, and I don't know how many more years I could realistically carry the load we've been managing at our property. I still need to find something that works for me though… something that helps pay the bills that is aligned with my livelihood and within my capacities."

"That's the spirit," Susan said, pouring two small cups of sake as she nodded. "Older, wiser, freer… tired."

Willow chuckled, "My body might be pleased if I just tend the food garden next summer. Half of the effort, half of the responsibility, half of the digging sounds just about right for these old bones. At the end of a long day, I feel like a decomposing heap…."

Susan passed Willow a sake cup. "To compost," Susan affirmed, raising her cup in a toast.

"Rot is hot," Willow said, as she gently touched her cup to Susan's and brought it to her lips while musing on her possible future.

As they came back up the stairs, Forest said, "There's something I want to show you. Be right back." He walked out to the truck and emerged from the cab with a hand-blown glass water pipe. "Wanna toke it in the gazebo?" Forest asked.

Spruce nodded and joined his son seated in front of their home. They looked out over the pond, nestled into a woven construction of willow reeds. Spruce had placed long willow branches into the ground and then interspersed the warping willow with wafting willow in a cylinder shape; the roof consisted of spiraling weaves coming to a point on high. A few small windows let light in from the north side, and a doorway looked out onto the pond.

"Nice bong kiddo. Your friend's work?" Spruce asked.

"Yeah, Jake gave me this one in trade for some of last summer's kush," Forest replied.

Swirled in fractal colors about the piece, shimmering blue trails merged with incandescent silvers. "I named her Lunazul," Forest added, installing the chosen selection of herbs into the bowl. Spruce passed Forest a lighter and a length of hemp twine. Lighting the end of the twine, Forest brought the burning tip to the bowl of pineapple buds. He inhaled and watched as the ignited crystalline flowers turned brown while the volatile parts of the plants were carried down the bowl stem into the main part of the bong. Bubbling up through a few cups of water, the smoke came back up the central channel of Lunazul where Forest had positioned his mouth to receive the smoke. Luxuriating in the first toke, Forest tasted the fresh flavors of the first hit.

"How's the pineapple express?" Spruce asked as Forest exhaled a mighty breath of fruity smoke.

"The best," Forest concluded, smacking his lips and passing Lunazul to his father. Spruce picked up the bong and set it on the table before him. He emptied the burnt buds into an ashtray and repacked the bong.

Willow arrived back on the homestead, bursting to get into the food garden. She had an elaborate meal plan brewing in her head that she had concocted on the drive home, inspired by her trip to the restaurant for lunch; she wanted to get out and collect her ingredients. When she pulled up, she found Forest and Spruce hot boxing the gazebo. She stuck her head into the opening, gestured for the bong, took a hit, smiled, nodded thanks, and headed out to the food garden.

She grabbed a basket from the front porch for harvesting as she sauntered by the cabin. She heard laughing echoing out over the pond from the gazebo, and she smiled as she unlatched the gate to her edible garden of earthly delights.

Stepping into the garden, Willow took a deep breath to allow the fresh fragrances of earth and vegetation to commingle in her nostrils. Her eyes softened their gaze as she let a palette of colors converge before her. Bright greens punctuated by the purples, magentas, oranges, and reds of fall dominated her field of vision, and she appreciated this repose from the rest of the world, frolicking in her own backyard. When Willow stepped into the garden, she was transported to a sanctuary of her own crafting. Her body relaxed, her lungs refreshed, and her mind calmed. She entered an altered state, dosed on the medicine of her healing co-creation with the plants. Her garden gate served both as a barrier to deer and a portal to another dimension.

Nothing compared in her mind to the beauty of her time spent in her open air playground. Hours turned to days turned to weeks turned to years spent here in this place, enticing growth to happen, flowers to flourish, and harvests to be abundant. Her intuitive faculties performed symphonic overtures with a panoply of plants on hand. Willow had fostered most of the plants in her garden from tiny seeds, blending spreading ground covers with berry-filled shrubs and fruiting trees with vines that reached their tendrils ever onward. Every space had been tended as she coaxed food forth from the leaves, stems, shoots, and seeds. While she conducted the affairs of this place daily, there were always surprises in the garden. Bird songs and bird poo had donated fodder for her fertile ground. Young compost tended to impart impish offerings of weeds as well. Some volunteers would be ripped away and fed to her animal familiars as she edited some improvised solos before they arrived at their full volume in her terrestrial orchestra.

And then suddenly her eyes came into focus, and she abruptly took several steps backwards to give some space to the rattlesnake she unexpectedly observed sunning next to her. "Helllllo," she said quietly, responding more to biology than to cognitive salutations. She gave her absolute and uncompromising attention to the snake on the ground. A single black tongue flicked in and out of the diamond-shaped head, and she was able to see that the snake was calm. She relaxed, letting the bird netting mesh come into focus, and she realized that there was a barrier between her and the snake. "Oh, you're stuck," Willow sympathized, watching the black tongue flickering in the undercover of the strawberry bed. She looked for the end of the bird netting and found it. "Let's get you out of here, eh?" The snake offered nothing much in way of a response, but continued to sense the scene with its tongue. Willow felt somehow that the snake was trusting her as she carefully untangled the netting while watching the rattler. She maneuvered until finally there was an opening and the front half of the rattlesnake was now exposed to the open air. "That's it! Go on then," Willow suggested, watching the rattler continue to remain calm. When the snake didn't budge, Willow looked around for a stick; she found something that would work nearby. From the back of the mesh, holding the netting up so that the snake wouldn't exit on her side of the mesh, Willow ever so gently began to softly push against the body of the snake. Although the rattlesnake didn't try to get out of the netting, it opened its mouth, fangs barred. No hissing issued forth, although its mouth remained agape. She stepped away, hoping that the snake would slither to safety. Why wasn't the snake moving? She had encountered many rattlesnakes in her day. Some of them would mosey along at the arrival of a human, and some of them were full of piss and vinegar and could rattle in a one snake percussion performance to beat the band. But this snake was impassive and almost too reserved. "You are a rattlesnake, aren't you? You've got that triangular head action. Not somebody else in disguise, right?" Willow started to wonder who she was dealing with in earnest because she was going to have to get a lot closer to cut the snake free from the netting, where she now saw its midsection seemed to be tightly wedged. "You're not calm. You're struggling, aren't you? I have to get you out of there. Fuck!" She shouted, "SPRUCE! FOREST!"

Plumes of smoke proceeded their exit from the gazebo. Father and son saw Willow waving them over with both arms, signaling distress. "HELP," she called out. Cupping her hands she added, "Bring the snake stick, NOW!"

Spruce broke into a jog, running and grabbing the stick from the front porch in one determined motion. Forest followed at his heels.

"SLOW!" Willow shouted as they got to the gate. "There's a rattlesnake and it's caught in the mesh bird netting."

From 60 to 0, the guys stopped just inside the gate. "Where?" They both asked in unison.

"It's right here, and it's stuck. I think we need to cut it free asap," Willow motioned them over. They came slowly to where Willow was standing and assessed the scene with fresh eyes.

"Dad, if you hold down the neck, I'll cut away the net from the body over here," Forest offered.

Spruce nodded, whipping out the multi-tool he carried around his belt and extending it to Forest.

"I'll hold and help pull away the netting," Willow added, since she was already holding the netting.

Feeling over the body of the tool, Forest used his nail to open the mechanism for the knife. It clicked into place. He took a deep inhale and asked around, "Ready?"

"Ready," Spruce replied.

"Ready," Willow said.

Spruce applied the fork of the stick to the back of the rattlesnake's head. Although it was not impossible for the snake to break free from, the maneuver would hopefully hold it until they were ready to move out of the way. Willow continued to hold the mesh tight so that Forest could see where to make the cuts. Having witnessed the snake stick go into position, Forest stepped down and made an incision along the length of the netting; when he got close enough to the body of the snake, he carefully cut perpendicular to the scales so that he didn't accidentally poke the rattler if it moved.

"There. It's open. It should be able to slither away now," Forest remarked, coming to a standing position.

"I'm going to let go of the netting, and get out of the way," Willow said and followed suit, standing next to Forest facing the tail end of the snake.

"Well, that leaves me," Spruce admitted. He watched the snake for a few more seconds from his parallel viewpoint. He looked to see where his family was, and he then turned his gaze back towards the snake while he simultaneously released the pressure on the stick and leaped away to the tail end of the snake.

Spruce landed, Willow reached out her arm to hold her stick wielder about his waist, and they all waited for the snake to move. Slowly, with its forked black tongue peeping through a mostly closed mouth, the rattler slithered out of the netting, along the path, through the gate, and away towards the orchards.

Willow sighed with relief and then said, "Thank you."

"You guys are still letting rattlesnakes do their own thing in your space?" Forest asked, remembering how his parents had coexisted with them on the land throughout his childhood.

"Pretty much. Although there's been an enormous king snake patrolling the strawberry patch for the last several days... so our liberated acquaintance might meet his demise in the garden anyway," Spruce answered.

"Yes, but that's not our fight. This however, was our bird netting and the onus of making it right was consequently on us. So, well done everyone! An untimely death has been averted, and I'm gonna fix up an amazing dinner now," Willow concluded as she picked up her harvesting basket.

Night

"What are you cooking up in here, mom?" Forest asked as he and Spruce walked into the house.

Seeing Willow bustling about, he wondered what inspiration his mother was following up on at full steam in the kitchen. Forest had long since moved away from his parents' homestead, preferring the bustling activity of the city. While he loved his parents deeply, being a gay man in the country had never quite suited him. As their official dealer, Forest came up from time to time to get more product to distribute; his parents rarely made it to the city to visit, although they did love having yummy nights out on the town at the restaurants in the Bay Area. During harvest, however, Forest came home and became their child all over again. He moved in for a few weeks, organized the trim crew, and dropped back into life on the land he knew so intimately from his upbringing.

Willow smiled as she continued to chop up her ingredients; pots were bubbling away on the stovetop and the oven was warming up to cook something delicious. "As I was eating my mushroom sushi today, I realized that the oyster mushroom crop was ready to be harvested," she said. "I am using the fresh mushrooms as the meat of the dish, incorporating them into a butternut squash sauce I just made with thyme, rosemary, garlic, and warming spices." While the men were visiting outside, Willow had made lasagna noodles from scratch; they waited on the kitchen table in full view ready to be layered into a deep dish Willow had oiled up.

"Smells delicious. Is it all from the garden?" Forest asked, always impressed with the level of engagement his parents had with their own food sustenance.

"I traded the olive oil for some goat cheese down in the valley. And we wildcrafted the walnuts from a friend's place over in Lake County. Everything else in this dish is homegrown," Willow replied, de-stemming chard and kale leaves with the precision of her knife blade.

Forest took a seat, and Spruce brought over three glasses to the kitchen table. "Pumpkin ale, also home-brew. Wanna glass?" Spruce asked.

Forest approved with a slight bow of his head, impressed by his parents' delicious repertoire, and Spruce poured their libations.

"Heard from your sister lately?" Spruce asked Forest as he passed his son a glass.

"She drops an email from time to time to say that she's still activist-ing with her non-profit like a social change globetrotter," Forest answered, taking a sip of the heady brew.

"She calls us about once a month to tell us how she's doing. Always trying to save the world that one," Spruce shared before sipping the brew too.

"Mmm! To world peace," Forest raised his glass.

"And delicious beer," Spruce added, toasting Forest's glass.

"I grew the hops," Willow interjected, reaching for a glass from Spruce with flour-covered fingers.

"Superior strobile sapidity, mom," Forest concluded, with beer foam bubbles tickling his upper lip beneath his moustache. "Last time Lily reached out to me she was in West Africa working at a refugee camp."

"Smoking weed in Ghana?" Spruce asked his son between sips.

"No doubt," Forest laughed.

When Forest and Lily were teenagers on the verge of college, Willow had arranged for a family trip for several months one summer to do volunteer work building an orphanage in Ghana. Spruce had stayed behind to tend the crop in Mendo, and the teens were surprised to find that there was a very vibrant weed community a world away. After landing in Accra for some capitol city life, the family trio had travelled to the coast, where they found themselves amidst shanty town cafes on the beach where the only menu item was an edible marijuana "space cake" dosed with Ghanaian chocolate (Ghana was then the world's number one exporter of cacao). The teenagers befriended several men who could roll joints with one hand in the darkest part of the night as they hung out on the beach, and Willow was impressed that she had chosen an expedition that delighted the kids. Spruce had received many postcards that summer about irie life on the islands as his family wrote about the surprising reality of being dropped into a Mendocino County doppelgänger in Africa.

"Maybe we could finally take your dad to Ghana," Willow chimed in, while layering the lasagna with slices of eggplant.

"Yes, we could go 'make fine in da bush' with dad after all these years," Forest chuckled, remembering the pidgin expressions the locals used for getting high in the sub-Saharan low growing shrubbery.

"I think Spruce would like the 'ghetto' too, don't you?" Willow joked with Forest who laughed out loud. Spruce had heard it all before of course, but one of the things that had shocked the teens the most on their summer trip was the way that the word "ghetto" had been used not in reference to a financially impoverished area where minorities were segregated but to a chill spot for smoking pot in the hidden rest areas constructed in the middle of swathes of African foliage. Willow held the line that pot was more of a visioning herb for adults while her kids were growing up, but by their teen years both of her kids had started to dabble in smoking pot and she eventually relented in her stoner parenting hoping that her kids' brains had developed enough to handle the substance without too much damage.

"He would love the ghetto! He could even set up his own hammock!" Forest howled with laughter, remembering how their weed-smoking West African friends had first showed them the "ghetto." While the family had initially been apprehensive, unsure what they might encounter at this ghetto, they were all much relieved when they realized it was actually just a couple of dudes reading books while they smoked joints in a human crafted nook. They visited the ghetto often on their trip, weaving their way among papaya trees, tall grasses, and diverse thicket plants.

Spruce smiled and said, "Maybe we could go next month?"

"A pot cultural exchange and post-harvest decompression vacay all in one!" Willow offered, as she placed the layered vegetable lasagna in the oven.

"And the men, dad. All. The. Men. Hold hands in Ghana. All the time. It's a thing of absolute beauty to behold," Forest remarked, fondly recalling how his formative coming out years were marked by the serene bliss of watching men regularly hold hands everywhere they went.

"Marcus would probably appreciate that too," Willow offered, wiping her hands on her apron and taking a sip of her pumpkin ale.

"Any gay man from America would probably find comfort in seeing that intimate social interaction of African men. It blew my young mind," Forest said, remembering the ease with which straight men reached for their comrades with open palms.

"How does Marcus feel about the legalization era?" Spruce asked before getting out the plates for their dinner.

"He's mixed. I think he's accepted that the economic flow that we have appreciated as a family business will taper off after this harvest," Forest said, getting the silverware out of the drawer.

"Will he miss the business itself?" Willow asked, tossing a salad at the counter.

Forest mused on the question for a moment, recounting the years of bringing pot to friends' houses and dispensaries with Marcus. He remembered many of the countless business interactions that they had made as a couple and the social network they had created predicated on trust, not contracts. "I'm gonna miss the business. It's in MY blood. I've known this trade my whole adult life."

Spruce reached over to massage his son's back, squeezing his strong shoulders.

"Marcus has said that he'll miss the verbal contracts and personal interactions of the pot trade. He feels like our operation as a profession far exceeds the usual capitalist job positions where you sell your soul to the company store," Forest continued, smirking.

"That's my son-in-law," Spruce laughed, folding napkins.

"But Marcus actually feels pretty positive about legalization. We've had a lot of discussions about how decriminalizing pot could mean a lot for people of color," Forest added, answering his parents' inquiry.

"Because black people are in jail for selling pot?" Spruce asked.

"That's part of it. If it becomes legalized, charges may be dropped for people serving time for crimes that are no longer criminal," Forest replied.

"What else?" Willow asked arranging the centerpiece on their table.

"Well, any time you have an issue that targets people of color, there's the reality of institutionalized racism. Yes, lots of black people smoke pot. But lots of other people smoke pot too. It's just that the system profiles and prosecutes the black folks far more than the others," Forest said, sipping his beer.

"So, in theory, legalization could potentially help acquit non-violent criminals from the prison industrial complex," Willow said, lighting a candle in the central wreath of the dining table.

"Let's hope so," Spruce said. "It's so wrong that people go to jail for this plant. So wrong."

"Yes. Any day we dismantle white supremacy as a society is a day of healing progress in my book! May this dramatic change in our lives be part of the dismantling of the overt discrimination people of color in America face. May the innocent be vindicated!" Willow said.

"Well, it'll either do that or make the rich bureaucrats' pockets fatter," Forest added. "Marcus and I aren't entirely sure that legalization will trickle down to the people who would actually benefit from having their cases absolved because the judicial system is slow, and the legalization of pot is still a jurisdiction issue."

"You mean, legal for who, where, and when?" Willow nodded, also weary of the consequences that legalization would entail.

"We're hoping that we're not just getting fired from our careers so that marijuana can be coopted by the large corporate interests hoping to centralize and capitalize on the economics of formerly illicit substances," Forest paused, shifting his mood from debating the issues to accepting the change more deeply. "But, like I said, we're out. Minorities are more vulnerable to everything, and we're not actually certain how the cards will play out. For us, with Marcus being black and us both being gay... plus wanting to adopt a child... things will be complicated enough without us being active in the drug trade, too."

CHAPTER 4

Thursday October 5, 2017

Morning

"Go Biodynamic," John suggested relentlessly. "Go Biodynamic and you'll expose yourself to a wealth of agriculture you only dreamed of so far. Besides, it's right up your alley, Spruce. You make your own compost already, and you try to keep your soil amendments coming from your farm in the form of animal manures and green fodder. You're a shoe-in."

Spruce had been meaning to talk to his friend about this alternative farming method for some time. Speaking into the landline, Spruce said, "You do have a beautiful farm John, and I totally respect where you're coming from as a farmer who walks his talk."

"Thank you. My farm has been my child of sorts, and I've invested my heart and soul in the land, for sure. I have a deep desire to spread this knowledge, and frankly I think this conversation is long overdue," John rallied on.

Spruce and Willow had met John during college at a Grateful Dead show in 1977. They were all students studying at University of California Berkeley, and John happened to be watching the concert next to them when he dropped acid; as a matter of good deadhead manners he offered Spruce and Willow some, and a lifetime friendship was immediately born midwifed by rock music and psychedelics. After completing their undergraduate degrees, the three headed up into the hills of Northern California on a field trip to participate in a burgeoning organic farm program before organic farms were popular. They spent the summer together getting a hands-on education in organics. After they finished their studies, they bounced around Northern California in a camper van, looking for their own plots of land. While volunteering at communities devoted to agriculture along the way, all three of them determined that they wanted to stay in the area to start their own earth-based initiatives. By the time Willow got pregnant with their daughter Lily, John had settled into a spot in Humboldt County where he was managing a pot grow; Spruce interned with John for a harvest before finding a lead on a place in Mendocino County. Although their paths had diverged when they both got their own lands in 1980, they still met up about once a year to share a meal or go on a hike. They pursued similar, parallel lifestyles but in their own respective locales.

"Yeah, I just don't know if we're going to keep doing our business. It seems like this is the last year for us and so many of our friends. The times, they are a changin," Spruce tentatively admitted.

"This is the answer! Biodynamics are a magical artistry on landscapes. At the very least you could apply some of the preparations to your food garden, and if you really do want to continue in the herb business, you could occupy a legal niche market in the dispensaries," John said, aware that he was one of the few pot farmers still able to sell his weed for a reasonable profit; he fully credited biodynamics with his success.

Spruce had been entertaining this new farming form for some time, and John had finally called him at the right time on the right morning to give him an earful of his suggestions.

"You take planting with the cycles of the moon and you add all this bonus material that helps create rich, diverse, alive soil. It's a win-win situation all around," John added.

"How long does it take to really understand how to 'go biodynamic'?" Spruce asked.

"Oh, Spruce, we're talking lifetimes to really integrate the material. You could read the 'Agriculture' lectures by Rudolph Steiner to ground you and give you a grasp of the basic provisions," John said.

"Hmmm… anything a little more direct? I mean, I'm happy to read anything. But if it's going to take lifetimes, it might be helpful to have more applied techniques. You know, so I can accomplish this feat while I'm still able to farm. You wanna mentor me?" Spruce wondered just how intense this information was going to be. He'd been gardening most of his life; could these methods really be so different?

"You can get started right away! I didn't mean to be off-putting. You can dig into esoteric science and keep digging and dig deeper still, that's all. It starts with grinding up some quartz crystals and burying cow horns full of poop, but it just gets weirder from there," John was on a roll.

"That all sounds pretty far out, John," Spruce smiled. "I can't believe I haven't gotten into it sooner!"

"You know what, the Biodynamics group gets together four times a year to meet up and make herbal preparations to apply to the soil. The folks discuss their methods and have a social meetup. The next gathering is around Winter Solstice up in Redwood Valley. It's practically in your backyard. We could go together, and I could introduce you to people who have been doing this forever; that way you could get your hands dirty," John said enthusiastically envisioning taking Spruce to the biodynamic meeting.

Just then, Willow completed her yoga morning session, stripped down to her birthday suit, and playfully returned to the house completely naked. Willow, for reasons she could not explain, found herself drawn to belly dancing while in the nude. This distracted Spruce completely from his phone call when he caught sight of her. She paraded across the homestead with the sunlight gleaming on her exposed skin, hips gyrating below and a load of dirty laundry balanced inside a basket on her head above. Spruce's eyes were glued out the window. After a moment's pause, he laughed aloud on the phone.

Confused, John asked, "Did I lose you?"

"Oh no, it's just laundry day. Go on," Spruce replied with a chuckle.

"I don't get it," John protested. "What's so funny about your laundry?"

"Willow just walked by naked, and I just realized that it must be laundry day," Spruce attempted to explain. "When we first got to the land thirty years ago we had to wash our clothes by hand. And so Willow got into doing naked summer laundry days. Since our clothes were all dirty, she could washboard everything with soapy water more easily if she was naked. It's still warm enough this fall for her to get away with a bare-bodied laundry morning."

"A Luddite?" John queried.

"Sometimes, in some ways. When the kids were born my parents got us a washer, but in all those years Willow never stopped having naked laundry days. Maybe it wasn't about the laundry so much as having an excuse to wander around naked," Spruce said, pleased with his wife's decision.

"Aha, a nudist," John replied.

"A part-time nudist on private property," Spruce admitted while sipping on his tea in his living room recliner.

"Let's talk again after the harvest, ok?" John urged. "I know the hills are a busy place at this time of year. In the meantime, I'll shoot you some articles about the science of biodynamics. The studies show just how drastic the soil improvements can be — even in areas with top soil depletion and erosion and environmental issues."

"Thanks John. I appreciate your support. That all sounds great," Spruce said. "I'll give you a call closer to the solstice."

"Fantastic! Have a great fall Spruce. Bye," John said, eager that he would be getting to reconnect with Spruce over agricultural adventures once more in the months to come.

After hanging up with John, Spruce floated on a cloud. He felt buoyed by his enthusiasm for novelty and intrigue and the possibility for great success. While Spruce had only the vaguest notion of what biodynamics actually meant, he did have a vetted trust of John's values for land-based stewardship. Where Spruce had started a venture with Willow on the land, John had created an impressively sustainable enterprise: cows grazed on holistically managed grasslands, draft horses carried plows, and an array of farm interns learned John's methods by tending dozens of acres of farmland. John had founded a CSA (community-supported agriculture) share program that brought fresh seasonal produce to families all over Northern California. John's farm teemed with biodiversity, and Spruce had often wished that they lived closer to each other so they could share ideas, extra seedlings, and dinners more often. Spruce didn't know what his study of biodynamics would yield, but he knew that he felt eager to participate in some of John's recipe for success firsthand.

Midday

Willow, now wearing a colorful sarong about her person, hollered for Spruce to come outside, "You've gotta see this, honey!"

Spruce walked outside to the storage shed area beside the barn. "Oh wow," Spruce admitted when he took in the scene. "Maybe it's time to consider visiting the animal shelter."

Before them lay a five-gallon bucket of fish emulsion, an organic fertilizer that they sometimes used in the garden, ripped open and drained of every drop of liquid. Spruce reached down and picked up the lid, which showed large teeth marks punctuating the top layer of plastic. As he waved it in the air, he remarked, "Seems to have slurped it down like a milkshake."

"A fish shake… ew, " Willow remarked, taking in the scene.

"Not gross if you're a bear. I've been wondering how long it would take for a bear to find us," Spruce said, shaking his head. "Maybe we could talk more about if it's the right time for us to bring a dog back into our lives."

"Oh Chestnut!" Willow wiped a tear from her eye as Spruce scooped her into an embrace.

Their family dog, Chestnut, had passed away in the past year, and they were still grieving the loss. They had gotten Chestnut when the kids were in high school and getting ready to go to college, to mitigate the empty nest syndrome that they had been told would afflict them.

"Come on, let's go bring some flowers to his grave," Spruce proposed.

As the couple walked through the garden harvesting a bouquet to take to Chestnut's grave, they were both quiet. The wound was still raw, pulsing with their memories of their beloved companion as they selected flowers from the different garden beds. They hadn't talked about getting another dog since Chestnut had passed away in their arms the previous winter. They'd had Ches his whole life; at fourteen years old his body stopped working, and he passed away quietly with the Wilder family all around him.

They took a path behind the house that led out toward the forest. Under a canopy of redwood trees, the couple held each other, letting the soft cool shade of the towering giants offer them comfort. Willow placed her bouquet of zinnias and calendula and forget-me-nots on Chestnut's burial site, which was delineated with stones and a small wooden arbor Spruce had built during the dog's last days. Spruce then placed his small bouquet of sunflowers and amaranth on another grave to the left of Chestnut's which marked the burial site of their dog Marvel, who had been a pup when the kids were babies and who had grown up alongside them on the ridge top.

"We've been so blessed by our canine family," Willow admitted, tears streaming down her cheeks.

"They are well worth our remembering," Spruce offered. "We have definitely been amazed by dogs. And, I think that it might be time to welcome a new member into the family."

Willow nodded. "Swim session discussion?" She asked while letting her sarong fall to the ground.

"Yes," Spruce said, taking in his beautiful naked partner before him. "But first, let's gather the essentials."

"I'll fix a salad if you bring the herbs," Willow proposed.

"Meet you at the pond in a few," Spruce said as he leaned in for a kiss. Squeezing Willow's hand, their lips met for a brief peck before they set out on their respective midday missions.

Spruce retrieved his herbal to-go kit, slipped off his clothing, and headed to the pond. When he got there, Willow had a picnic basket in hand. They both got onto a wooden raft that the couple had made for fun when the kids were younger, loaded up their goods, and headed to the island in the middle of the pond. Similarly, the island had been a project that the couple had taken on with the kids, making a floating bit of land anchored in the middle of the pond for them to dock on during their summertime swims. Over the years they had experimented with having ducks live on the island, but these days they just used the space as their chill lounge in the summertime. Spruce secured the raft to a post at the edge of the island as Willow laid out her sarong for the couple to sit on. She plopped down with the go-to kit in hand and began to roll up a joint for them to enjoy.

"What appetizer do we have here?" Willow asked Spruce while breaking up the herb in a metal grinder in preparation for rolling.

"We're going to be smoking 'OG Strawberry Diesel' today," Spruce said, handing her a small envelope of hemp rolling papers.

"It's times like these I'm so glad we are the last house at the end of the road," Willow said just before she raised the joint in progress to her mouth to run her tongue along the sticking edge. In one smooth motion she used her finger to seal the moistened paper over itself, forming a long thin cylinder of garden fresh Ganga ready to be ignited.

"It was certainly less expensive to be more remote; and who knew that we could have the fringe benefit of being able to lounge in the nude?" Spruce smiled, passing Willow a lighter.

"I want to toast our lives out here with this strawberry doobie. We have been able to support ourselves in our line of work for a very long time, and I am grateful," Willow said igniting the joint.

After luxuriously inhaling the fruity flavors, Willow passed the joint to Spruce.

He added, "I want to toast to our lives together out here. We have everything we could ever want. We have a beautiful place to call home, clean water, land to live by, and the best company in all the world." He inhaled deeply and they both relaxed a little more into gratitude as the herbs imbued them with a changed perspective.

"I do want to open the door for a dog to come into our lives," Willow finally declared.

"I wasn't sure if Ron would keep the wildlife at bay with his gun. I thought it was possible," Spruce mused about his gun-toting neighbor who lived on the next parcel over. "But that fish emulsion got tanked, and if the bear's coming around for that it might not be long before the orchard and the chickens need more protection too."

"Ron's good at shooting, and any animal with any sense within several miles should stay clear. But that's not always how it works. Bears and mountain lions get hungry and top of the food chain predators can afford to get bold," Willow remarked, remembering countless tales from their time on the ridge and previous encounters with large wild animals.

"Yes, we've always had a dog," Spruce nodded and passed the joint back to Willow.

"This year has been such a whirlwind. The economic flux from the pot industry has been so very distracting, and my thoughts have been preoccupied with what is going to come next for us," Willow said before she took a long draw from the joint in her hand. Exhaling slowly, she said, "When Chestnut passed I just couldn't go there yet, even though I knew that we needed a dog with us on the land. It was all just too much."

"Chestnut was the perfect dog for us, and we were pretty good people to her too," Spruce added.

"Absolutely," Willow agreed as she passed the joint back to Spruce. "But more than that, I just wasn't sure what our future was going to hold. I still don't know what our future is going to hold, but I think that it's clear that we thrive living on this land."

"You weren't thinking we would move, were you?" Spruce asked while taking a puff.

"I didn't know. I don't know. If you take marijuana out of the equation, there's a lot of gaps and holes in my logic around where I want to be and what I want to be doing," Willow said as Spruce passed the joint back to her. She shook the ash off the joint and articulated, "Without Mary Jane tying us to the ridge top, what's possible for us?"

Spruce's jaw had truly dropped now. He sat there befuddled, unclear how to process what Willow had just shared.

"I mean, a part of us lives in this land no matter what. We're here and as much as we can be from a place as white people on the land we are married to the ridge top," Willow allowed. "But what if we wanted to go traveling or explore working social justice issues or... I don't know Spruce. I just know that we're at a crossroads and if we're going to be here, then it makes every bit of sense to find ourselves as doggy parents again. If we're going to start a new chapter, I just want to talk more about what this chapter might look like and how we might see ourselves evolving into it."

"I know what you're saying. I know we're shifting something really huge. We have three decades of commitment to homesteading that we've been riding on, and rather abruptly the laws of physics have changed," Spruce acknowledged.

Spruce and Willow, dipping their toes into the truth of their present situation, felt both afraid to dive into something new as adults. Confused, they wondered how they could reinvent themselves. While the Wilders carried a wealth of information and resources with them into whatever endeavor they might approach, they also had never had to take on such a huge career genesis. They had wandered into cultivating herb out of necessity and convenience. Over the years it had become more than just a job to them; they were able to creatively express themselves, sustain their livelihood on the ridge top, and pay all their bills with a net profit left over. The task at hand, though daunting to anyone, hit them doubly hard since they both had chosen the same career; likewise, they were both asked by circumstance to evolve in a way that neither of them had any practice doing.

"I have been talking with friends in our same situation. We're getting older and we're still going strong now, but how much longer can we run a homestead by ourselves?" Willow wondered. "How much longer do we *want* to run a homestead by ourselves? I mean, it's all good fun naked swimming and gardening out here as dinosaurs of the Wild West, but the Wild West is changing. We can't keep paying our property taxes with weed money. We don't even know if we can sell the weed we're bringing in right now. It's just… terrifying," she said as she passed Spruce the joint again.

Spruce nodded. "I hear you. But we will pay the property taxes this year. For next year, we're gonna have to get more creative."

"I want to stay, and I want to get a dog. I just want to be able to mention these things as they come up so that we don't feel totally broadsided by the very real changes that are happening to us and in us," Willow rallied.

"Well, it's important to be open," Spruce agreed, taking a puff. "Especially with Forest and Marcus seriously considering adoption… If we had grandkids in Oakland, we might think twice about living at the last house at the end of the road in the Mendo hills."

Willow's face lit up in a million shades of grandmother joy. She squealed with delight, throwing her back onto the sarong so that her legs kicked up into the air while she made elated noises. Spruce laughed to see her response. They both were reveling in Forest's news, and Spruce knew that the prospect of being grandparents would soften some of the intense processing that they were navigating.

Willow recovered her wits and said, "Well, yes, it's good to keep our options open!" She sat up, looking out over their glassy pond. "I'm ready for a swim." With that, she dove into the pond, making a splash.

Spruce joined her to cool off; together they moved through the aquatic plant life, tickled by the small fish nibbling at their toes. They floated on their backs, letting the whole body of water overtake them. With their ears under the water, the quiet sloshing of the pond poured through them, calming their nerves and relaxing their brains. As Spruce lingered, becoming one with the pond, Willow returned back to the picnic basket on the island and got out a knife. Holding it between her teeth, blade out, she swam out to the edge of the pond.

For years the couple had introduced different things into the pond as scientific experiments. The ducks had been a good source of eggs, but they had made the island more duck poo than lounge area. So after some further consideration, the couple had made duck soup. Spruce had brought in water lilies which still floated about here and there, offering a beautiful lotus bloom from time to time. Willow had planted willow along the edges, and Spruce had filled the gaps in the willow sections with cattails. Today Willow harvested cattails, cutting down at the bottom of the plant where the long green tails all joined in a singular white stalk. When she had harvested about ten stalks, she said thank you to the cattails, gathered the bundle, and swam back with it towards the island.

As Willow separated the cattail fronds into pieces, Spruce swam back up to the island and opened the picnic basket. Willow used her knife to cut sections of the juicy white cattail and put them on a plate that Spruce put next to her for that purpose. The couple enjoyed the tender shoots as their first course.

"So refreshing," Willow said of her first bite, and then she continued to break up the stalks and lay them out on the island to dry.

"Making a hat?" Spruce asked aloud, knowing well that Willow had a tenacious weaving hobby.

"Probably," Willow admitted. In the barn there were several such hats already, waiting for guests to use on sunny days in the garden.

As Spruce continued to empty out the picnic basket, the spread that Willow prepared grew to occupy much of their sarong space.

They both heard a splash at the other end of the pond. They immediately turned to see what was stirring, but all that remained as evidence was a small ripple slowly diffusing across the surface of the pond.

"I've been wondering about otters lately," Spruce admitted.

"It's been a while since I've seen any of them up here," Willow said.

"I know. But they might still use this pond as a waterway on their wildlife corridor," Spruce said, still studying the spot where the ripple had been.

"Yes, I suppose you're right. Why, are you still thinking about the beaver lecture?" Willow asked, curious.

"Have you ever felt a beaver pelt?" Spruce turned and smiled at Willow.

"Is that an eco-sexual pick up line?" Willow returned with a smile.

"Maybe," Spruce paused. Willow laughed and continued to arrange their lunch dishes and cutlery.

"Wasn't the keynote of that presentation that beavers were most valuable alive?" Willow pointed out.

"Yes, alive and doing beaver things in the waterways. Absolutely. But, the linchpin in the presentation was that beavers have amazing pelts," Spruce countered.

"Indeed. They were so amazing that the fur trade nearly wiped out the California beaver populations. Beaver pelts apparently turned into many felted hats," Willow remembered, thinking back on the lecture and slideshow they had seen a few weeks before at the Environmental Center in Ukiah. "We love everything to death in a consumer culture, don't we?"

"Close. Not entirely. Although their numbers have declined steadily, there are still pockets of beaver throughout California," Spruce chimed in. "Beaver pockets," he repeated with emphasis.

"Is it because I'm high that everything seems like a sexual innuendo right now?" Willow asked.

"High. Naked. On an island contemplating beavers," Spruce said. "Sounds like a fine day, if you ask me."

"I thought we were contemplating otter routes of passage, actually," Willow pursed her lips, bemused by the afternoon palaver.

"Wait for it," Spruce said. "If we don't have otters coming through here anymore, I was thinking about introducing a beaver to the pond area. Our own little beaver pocket."

Willow had had many experiences with Spruce's hunches and experiments on the homestead. Often they were educational, and sometimes they were more difficult to extract a lesson from…

"You want to illicitly relocate a beaver into our pond?" Willow summarized, handing Spruce a bowl of salad.

"I was talking to some friends after the talk, and it's kinda becoming a thing," Spruce admitted, taking the salad. "Thank you."

"It was a very good presentation," Willow smiled, "Did you have a plan as to where exactly you were planning to procure said beaver?"

"The 'slow it, sink it, spread it' guys have been doing it. Permaculture activists have their ways," Spruce replied confidently.

"Really? Doing what? Stealing large rodents for environmental purposes?" Willow asked, but then followed, softening, "Why not? We could all use more beavers in our lives, couldn't we?"

"That's the beaver spirit," Spruce laughed aloud.

Night

Spruce and Willow left their well-lit cabin to emerge in the outdoors where the moon shone brightly overhead. They allowed the unveiling of the light to unfold before them as their eyes adjusted to the transformation of their visual sense, their pupils widening. Summoning faculties from their ancestors before the advent of electricity, the Wilders awakened their night vision, letting the natural elements of the moon and stars serve as their lantern. They perceived more and more of their surroundings as they held hands on their front porch. As the minutes passed, their acuity increased steadily, and before long they were well able to navigate their way through their homestead with alacrity. Grabbing some tools from the porch, they headed out on a nighttime walk to a spot in the woods. Spruce struck the ground with his copper shovel, moonlight glinting off the concave shovel head as he dug out the first load of earth.

"Full moon on high tonight," Willow commented, seeing the light reflected on their gardening tool.

"Perfect time to bury money in the ground," Spruce joked.

"Lunar banking at its best," Willow joined in, laughing.

Spruce continued to take load after load of dirt out of the hole, stacking it in a mound next to where they intended to bury their canister.

"Do you ever think we've gone wacky, burying our money in the ground? Maybe as farmers we're taking our relationship to the ground a little too far?" Willow asked fiddling with the army canister in her hands.

"Unless you want the feds coming after you for suddenly depositing several thousand dollars into a bank account for which you have no traceable income on file, I think burying it in the ground is brilliant," Spruce replied, nodding to Willow that he was ready for her part of the burial.

Willow maneuvered the container with their previous year's savings into the ground. "And so it is; it is done!"

Filled with bills wrapped into spiraling packets, further wrapped in waterproof packing and then fitted into old army canisters, Willow and Spruce had their savings for the last 30 years peppering the land outside their home in several shallow holes. Most of their money went to living on the land; however, $100,000 had been parceled out into these storage containers. Not enough to retire on but enough to help them along for many years, their buried wealth awaited further plans underfoot. Willow took out a notebook and indicated on a map of their home where the newest container had been buried. She looked up and nodded to Spruce.

"Did you hear something?" Spruce asked, and around the corner of the barn, six yards away a family of raccoons scuttled by.

"Out for an evening stroll," Willow surmised, watching the mother raccoon lead her kids across the meadow toward the forest. She paused to remember if she had gotten all her chickens into their pen that evening. Although the raccoon family had a sweet demeanor from their human perspective this evening, they had been bloody murderous when it came to their poultry pets.

Looking up at the full moon, Spruce noticed, "Good lighting! Glad we can see them without any flashlights to scare them off."

They watched the modest parade go on until the family was under the cover of trees and they became shadows in the night.

"I wonder how complicated biodynamics would be to apply to our gardens. Besides planting by the moon, do you know what it takes to get certified?" Spruce asked Willow, using the shovel to cover the canister in the ground.

"I think they bury things by the moon too. Cow horns filled with manure or quartz crystals or both," Willow said.

Spruce looked concerned. "What?"

"This reproof from a man who a few hours ago was ready to begin the beaver import business? And who just buried his fortune underground!" Willow chided Spruce's facial expression. "I think that you're in no position to rule out anything that might be part of the solution at this point in the game, Spruce Wilder. Besides, the freakier the answer these days, the more I like it. The world's gone to pot, but not the smoking kind, and you would do better to delay your disbelief until you explore the boundaries of your inquiry further."

Spruce nodded. "John's produce always tastes amazing. For years I've been trying to get him to give me recipes from his kitchen, but he always insists it's just the quality of the produce from biodynamic methods."

"In general, I think that the method has more to do with the use of materials from the farm on the farm than anything else. You know: a holistic environment. And I think that we'd be growing non-psychotropic herbs to make the 'preparations' with, too," Willow added.

"John mentioned making our own composts," Spruce remembered.

"It's always better to make your own. Grow your own food. Build your own compost to improve the soil. Return what you use back to the earth. I don't really know, but I think biodynamics takes that to the next level. Could be interesting to implement," Willow shrugged.

Spruce tapped his foot over the buried canister, evening the dirt layer on the surface level. "I do strive to have a full circle with the farm inputs and outputs. I think that's why I get so vexed about the possibility of a corporate pot takeover. It's bad enough that big business would be profiting from herb. But it really drives me mad when I think about the extractive nature of conventional agriculture practices," Spruce said, perched next to the shovel, gesticulating to Willow in the moonlight.

"Well, lots of growers are already in the extractive nature of the business. Gangsters and mafia dudes set up illicit grows in the National Forest all the time. They pour toxic fertilizers into the wild lands which seep into the groundwater, further contaminating the ecosystem. Then they take the plants and leave a big mess. They extract the wealth already, honey," Willow reminded him.

"Yes, and you know how that drives me mad," Spruce said walking with the shovel towards the barn.

Willow followed, equally frustrated with the lack of accountability among some of their competition.

"I mean, what is it going to take to make changes? Greed seems to be driving this round of legalization. I do not doubt that there are probably some benefits to legalizing pot, but I fear that the legislative shifts have more to do with bigger extractive businesses than with civil rights changes. When is need going to galvanize minds? When is the need for clean air and clean water and healthy land going to motivate people? How much longer will this gravy train ride into the horizon?"

"I think that the train stops here. We can't keep burying money in the ground. It's a short-term solution for a long-term issue. We need to have a better sense of security for our golden years, Spruce. We need to shift away from something that the government can come after us for. We have no guarantee that the world isn't going to heat up beyond repair within our lifetimes. We can grow our own foods and live lightly on the land. We cannot stop the government from trying to take it all away if we keep growing pot," Willow said, propelled by grief to speak more reasonably about their future.

"We have no insurance. We have no retirement. It's all in the land. Literally, in the ground, and above ground as well. We have a legacy to protect and weed has become a bigger adversary than it is an asset anymore. We have what we have, and we need to guard it fiercely," Spruce agreed.

"No insurance. I just wish we could change that. Are we absolutely sure we can't get any insurance?" Willow asked Spruce.

"To become legal grow, our site would need to be checked. We live in a totally renegade scene as far as the building department is concerned," Spruce concluded. "Permitting is just not an option. It would require thousands of dollars up front to have the garden be recognized as legally legitimate. It's too risky to have the house reported and red tagged. We'd owe the building department a ton of money. I mean, none of our structures are to code, and I don't know how forgiving they would be… a house, a barn, a pond… they're all clandestine creations at present. Presuming we were even able to get permitted, we still might not be able to get an insurance policy on the house and outbuildings. I think our best bet is investing in something that doesn't draw so much attention to the homestead."

"And in protecting the homestead passionately," Willow added. "Since we have no insurance and we're not going to be able to get any home insurance, we've got to keep taking more measures to fortify the land from attack."

"That's the thing. We can do lots of things to protect our space ourselves as sovereign stewards. But we can't really afford to try to get our place up to code and go the legal, normal route. I'm pretty certain that the house is not going to pass inspection. It'll survive most anything, so they might give us amnesty, but they might not. For that point alone I keep coming up against the reality that we are gonna have to stop growing. If they really do catch up with their own legislation around legalization protocols, they are gonna start cracking down hard on anyone not in compliance with the permitting procedures. The black market is under more scrutiny than ever before. And that alone could cost us the homestead. Rather than get slapped with fines for doing everything illegally, I think that we could truly finish up the season and slide under the radar. Even if we do end up getting busted by building and planning folks at some point, it will be much easier to navigate their protocols without a grow scene happening," Spruce said, considering the bureaucratic malaise of what it would take for them to become more transparent and accountable on the books.

"Well, we've avoided the backwoods shoot 'em ups this long," Willow said. "Let's hope getting out now will fend off future altercations."

"It's going to be the law that's going to be the one coming for growers and starting a ruckus from now on," Spruce said. "Not rival gangs or looters or vigilante groups. The full backing of the powers that be are looming stronger than ever before."

"So we need to get out there and make our space more defensible," Willow continued.

"From the law?" Spruce asked.

"From the elements," Willow replied. "We're hoping to skirt the law."

"Take the money and run," Spruce chuckled.

"Take the money and bury it," Willow corrected. "But that's just one part. We have gotten what we can from the ganga economy. After we finish up this harvest, we need to really look at creating a more secure homestead."

"I've been thinking about what it would take to install a moat," Spruce commented.

Willow, envisioning King Arthur and dragons lurking under water, asked for clarification, "To keep the bandits out? Or the post-apocalyptic roving zombies? You lost me."

"None of the above necessarily, but I like your imagination. I was thinking about fire. To keep out wildfires from taking our home," Spruce answered.

"Like a water moat with a drawbridge? I'm only seeing castles in my mind's eye. How are you figuring you'll apply this to the ridge top?" Willow wondered aloud.

"I heard about a farm over in Lake County where a fire came through and burnt down all of their buildings. However, they had a watered front yard garden, a pretty big zone right in front of their door that extended down the path for half an acre. When they came back after the fire was put out, their home was in ashes, but their lettuce was still fresh in the garden. The wetness of the garden immobilized the fire. Problem is, the fire wrapped around the other sides of the house and took their building down. But what if we could build a garden moat that ran on grey water for a couple of yards around the house in all directions?" Spruce explained his theory.

"A moat," Willow reflected.

"A plant moat," Spruce affirmed.

"No beavers?" Willow joked.

"Not in the moat," Spruce smiled. "But, they're part of the holistic team to keep the land healthy. It takes a village. We've taken down the trees right near the house, and we need to keep the brush down. I think that the moat would really take it to the next level. I'd feel a lot safer about our situation with a moat. The more defensible we make our space, the better chance we have of keeping it."

"We need to be our own insurance policy," Willow concluded, yawning. "I think it's time for bed."

The weary Wilders brushed their teeth, musing on the paradigm shifts ahead of them. Willow splashed cool water on her face, and Spruce gargled spring water from the bathroom faucet. As they crawled into bed, both snuggled up close, curled up in a loose tangle of human bodies under the fluffy down comforter. While the October temperatures during the day continued to stay warm and dry, the evenings dipped down into the 40s and 50s. Cuddling, although always appreciated for intimacy, became employed as the customary sleeping arrangement from the fall equinox onward. Although the Wilders lived in California, they inhabited a cooler region than many of their sunny state counterparts. From the tree cover surrounding the Wilder's cultivated home, the twelve hundred foot elevation, and the less intense angle of sunshine in October, the ridge top property tended toward cold nights.

As the Wilders warmed each other, they drifted off to sleep. Spruce closed his eyes while designing his garden moat, visualizing what plants would go where in his mind; the real imagery turned from revery to fantasy and took him to dreamland. Willow fell asleep almost instantly, her body truly tired from a day working hard on the land. With heavy eyelids pressing down, Willow's consciousness played between her waking commitments on the homestead and a more fanciful journey through her slumberland.

Willow's suddenly walking through the forest, stepping cautiously over pine needles and cold pebbles. Bioluminescent mushrooms are blooming on both sides of her feet, pouring over the trail, lighting her way. She turns when she hears rustling in the woods, indicating to her that she is not alone; out of the corner of her eye she sees glowing eyes staring in her direction. But there's another light, straight ahead of her, that's calling to her. It's small, so she keeps moving ahead, hoping that the light will come into focus. As she continues on the path, she realizes that she is a young girl because her hands are small and the world around her feels magical. In the light ahead of her she can just make out a fire someone is tending. Willow moves her bare feet slowly off the path, preferring to move under cover of darkness between the trees; she turns to check on the glowing eyes behind her and they, too, have moved off the path. She slips under madrone branches, letting her palm feel the cold, smooth bark as she maneuvers closer to the light ahead. A cloud of bats flies overhead, skirting around trees as they too navigate through the nighttime forest. As the bonfire comes into sharper focus, a parade of animals scurries out from the surrounding woods to watch the proceedings. Willow feels the hairs on the back of her head extend out, sensitive to the vibrations of movement from behind her; she breathes in deeply, pivots slightly in her slippers, and sees the shadowed form of a mountain lion striding toward her. Willow's eyes widen as the feline form stands as tall as the girl herself, and their eyes lock as they meet. The mountain lion nods and Willow gently lets her head curtsy as well.

Following the gigantic cat comes a parade of coyotes, foxes, skunks, raccoons, squirrels, and mice. Their numbers swell, and she finds herself holding onto a madrone branch to ground herself from the onslaught; the tree she's grasping subtly shakes as owls, woodpeckers, and hawks silently fill the upper branches, perching on high. Little Willow sees the masses teeming closer and closer to the fire; she continues to stalk on her own quiet feet until she stands in the ring of trees circling around the outside of the bonfire. The animals weave in and out of the trees too, until everyone has situated themselves, looking towards the center.

There an old woman with a cloth woven around her head is adding wood to the burn, placing each branch with care. She's formed a tall pyramid of flames, with precisely staked logs radiating out from the uppermost peak where all the wood converges and the light travels up. Willow studies the old woman's features as they shine in the light of the fire. She's so close that she can see the oak bark on the logs that the crone is placing into the firepit. Enchanted by the light, Willow carefully walks closer to the fire and the curious elder; the animals come in closer too, until they are all able to hear the crackling of the oak logs burning hot in the fire pit.

Carefully, the old woman wipes her hands on her apron and smiles at the child. Willow cannot decide if she likes the smile or if she should run. She feels suddenly uncertain about why she has gotten so close to this woman in the woods. As she wonders, the wood spits and a hot coal jumps out and burns a hole in Willow's dress before she shakes it off. But the enchantment is broken, and Willow sees now that the old woman is laughing and that she has mounted onto an enormous mortar that Willow didn't notice before. The smell of her burning outfit brings her even more into the clarity that she has wandered into the wrong part of the woods.

Then the woman's old hands clap together, reverberating as the animals all begin to flee helter skelter away from the bonfire in all directions. The mountain lion's eyes glow bright and gaze at Willow for a fraction of a second before she jumps onto the cat's back, arms tight around the neck. The woman has grabbed the enormous pestle now and is starting to fly above the bonfire. Willow cranes her head back to see the witch cease her cackling, bring her lips together, inhale a vast breath, and blow. Rising up above the tree line, the witch continues to blow, while Willow and the lion make their way out of the woods and to the oak meadows. As they break through the trees to the open sky, Willow sees the old woman on high, breathing bigger and bigger breaths into the fire. Willow can't actually tell if the woman is simply blowing onto the fire or if she is actually breathing fire because the bonfire has grown, and the forest is now fully aflame. Looking back at the inferno, Willow gasps at the immensity of the wildfire in the woods and loses her grip on the lion's neck. She hits the ground, rolling down the hill and wakes up in a hot sweat, falling off her bed.

"Ouch," Willow breathed quietly, taking stock of where she was and what was happening.

"Are you okay?" A groggy Spruce asked, peering over the side of the bed while pulling down the bedside light chord.

Willow paused, assessed her waking state and determined that she wasn't running from a fire. "I just had a really intense dream, I think." She sat up, taking in the sensation of the sheep skin she had fallen onto beneath her and gripping the side of the bed to pull herself up. "The forest's not on fire?"

Spruce gazed out the window for a moment through squinting eyes before saying, "Looks clear to me."

Noticing aches on her hips and back, Willow gently moved her body back onto their bed, testing for sore spots as she landed. "Baba Yaga," she mouthed.

Spruce, still not fully awake, murmured, "The witch?"

"Yes, the witch from my Russian grandmother's stories. You remember? The one who eats children and flies around in a mortar and pestle."

"The one that lives in a cabin in the woods atop gigantic chicken feet?" Spruce said, more awake now, rubbing Willow's back gently as they both sat up in bed.

"She was calling all the forest animals to her, but then we all had to run for our lives because she was breathing fire. I rode a mountain lion to safety," Willow remembered the vividness of the dream.

"Were you lucid?" Spruce asked, wondering how conscious the dream had been for Willow. "Do you remember what happened, or has it slipped away?"

"Somewhat. It felt like we were all enchanted by her; but as I got closer to the bonfire I woke up in the dream and realized I had to leave quickly. Still, I was drawn to that flame, and it was difficult to look away," Willow admitted.

"But you made it out and the animals too?" Spruce checked.

"Yes, we all made it out… but the forest burned down. Where would we go, and what would we do if our house was suddenly taken by flames?" Willow asked Spruce.

"Let's hope we never have to find out."

CHAPTER 5

Friday October 6, 2017

Morning

As the sun crested the hilltops in the east, the ridge came alive with the fiery colors of the dawn. Birds sang their melodies, the weed stretched slightly toward the light of the new day, and the grasses swayed in golden patches all along the length of Redwood Valley.

"The last Wilder family crop of weed. I thought I'd be a very old man, doobie in hand, before I had to see this day come to pass. How many other families are in our position?" Spruce asked Willow as they stayed in bed longer than usual to discuss the day's logistics.

"I'd say a good deal of Northern California is having this exact conversation this season," Willow admitted. "Or permutations on the theme of how are we going to support ourselves now with the cost of pot bottoming out?"

"This is it, isn't it? We're getting out of the pot business," Spruce said, still struggling to stop his resistance and accept their decision.

"We're finally firing ourselves," Willow said, snuggling under the covers. She turned to Spruce and mused, "wanna hire ourselves for something else?"

"Maybe we could grow mushrooms," Spruce interjected. "Because once you go illegal, it's hard to go legal?" Willow said, rolling her eyes, and she pulled the blankets up a little more so that the comforter came up to her neck. The cool autumn mornings had arrived, even if the rains were still nowhere in sight.

"No, I mean mushrooms like oysters and shiitakes. Which reminds me, I need to check on the inoculated logs today. Might be time to bring on a storm," Spruce hopped out of bed.

"I need to check the trimmer room today too, to make sure we have all the chairs and bins and clippers in there," Willow followed suit, itemizing their day's chores.

As Spruce pulled on his jeans, he said, "We could always grow other plants on the land. What about growing food to sell at the farmer's market? It would be a different income bracket, but we would still be able to get our hands dirty and offer organic or maybe even biodynamic produce to the community."

"Anything that allows me the freedom to work at home and exist outside of the nine to five reality sounds like a win. But even if we can't pull that off, I'm grateful that we were self-employed on our own terms for so long," Willow admitted, finally opening the bedcovers to begin her day in earnest.

"Totally," Spruce agreed. "What about creativity and art and time for other expressions to come through? When your nose is to the grindstone, even the luxury of musing about another way of life must feel daunting. As long as people are kept in a kind of subsistence servitude, there is a serious limit on the creative power that can come through; there are only so many hours in a day."

"I think Mendocino County is having a transformation, and I'm not sure how it's going to shake down. But I know that the economics are going to get crunchy. We haven't had to work multiple jobs to keep our heads above water. We were able to graduate college, buy land, and raise our kids with a lot of free time on the land. I don't know how people are going to be able to afford land in this county anymore," Willow said, opening her dresser drawer. A loud shot resounded in the background. "Guess Ron's at it again. Maybe that'll keep the bears at bay until we get a dog." Willow pulled a long cotton shirt over her head.

"It feels like a lot of work to me to get a puppy during harvest. Do you think we should hold off until after the crop is in?" Spruce asked, aware that their fall homesteading operation was about to expand while they harvested and trimmed their final herb crop.

"Oh my, the puppy responsibility is daunting… but maybe the trimmers could help socialize the pup and take on some of the pup's needs as part of their work shifts?" Willow suggested.

"Let's see if they're animal people. And if there's a dog lover or two in the group, then I'd be open to that," Spruce offered. "Otherwise, let's start searching as soon as we finish the trimmer scene."

"Great," Willow agreed, pulling on a pair of yoga pants. "Remember how we talked about firming up our evacuation plans? I think that this is the last morning to get everything in place before the crew arrives. It would be good to review our process before we have to describe it to them."

"Do you ever feel like we're a little too obsessed with fire?" Spruce asked.

Willow, now fully clothed, stared out their bedroom window, silently considering his question before she concluded, "Better to be prepared. There's only the one way out."

"Down," Spruce agreed.

"The fire this summer came too close. While I think that we weren't complacent before, I don't think that we can ignore the threat anymore. We know too much about California fire ecology. We know too much about the lack of forest management. We know too much about what a real, formidable, and overwhelming threat an unexpected fire poses for our survival," Willow replied.

"It wasn't that long ago that Lake County went up in smoke either. All it takes is one spark at the wrong time to change the landscape. Remember ten years ago that dry lightning storm in June? We couldn't see down the driveway from all the smoke," Spruce remembered the unprecedented lack of visibility for over a week at the ridge top ranch.

"Collectively, we're still trying to suppress fire. Until we start burning thoughtfully, and as long as we keep building homes in the fire zones we're screwed unless we have a strong plan. I doubt that we're going to see anything more this season, as we've already had our scare. But in the years to come, as the drought intensifies with global warming, we're going to have to be more vigilant about our plans."

"So I suppose we're appropriately obsessed. Why isn't everybody else though? I mean, we have friends that are creating fire-defensible spaces, but mostly I get the sense that people would rather pretend that this isn't an issue," Spruce finally answered his own question.

"Mostly, I think people are too busy to do what it takes to make the overarching changes necessary with regard to fire. And if they do have the time, they're too out of touch to understand just how precarious our modern ways are. I think that it's going to take something truly cataclysmic to wake people up. And once they're aware of the threat, it's going to take some serious changes to really remedy the problem."

"Fire's not the problem. Our lack of intelligence with regard to working with fire is the issue. And our lack of management could become truly dangerous. Maybe not today, maybe not for years. But all it takes is one false move by us or somebody else to test the limits of the system."

"I'll make sure that the sprinklers are spread out around the outside of the house," Willow offered.

"I'll check that the mobile pump is still working down by the pond," Spruce said, listing off their errands.

"I'll double-check that the fire hose is wound up correctly in the box," Willow continued. "We might have been sloppy after that scare in July."

"I'll make sure that the four-wheeler is full on gas," Spruce added.

"There's not enough time for the plant moat to be put in place, but our list is pretty thorough nonetheless," Willow said, half teasing Spruce about his long-term project.

Spruce laughed out loud as they both headed outside.

While the Wilders kept themselves busy bustling about their property to prepare for Forest's arrival, the ladies of perpetual psycho-activity were holding court in their garden beds. Each plant had grown in a large pot which had been mixed to contain the right amount of nutrients in a substrate of healthy, balanced soil. Few plants were ever planted directly into the ground when it came to marijuana cultivation. With so much riding on the success of these plants, the potted enclosures ensured that all the additions were being carefully maintained. Water allotments and fertilizer feedings were administered in ratios deemed maximally effective by the growers. Pots could be moved around if necessary to optimize growth patterns, sun exposure, and spatial awareness between the different potted plants. Not unlike a well-bred dog competing for best in show, these plants had been domesticated and pampered to produce the finest specimens. They were regularly fawned over, petted, and inspected for premium progress. Their development schedule was closely guarded, since any mishaps required immediate intervention and increased attention.

October marked the crowning glory of the growing season. Plants in a five-hundred-mile-wide radius had achieved flowers and were ready to be plucked. Unlike a garden of sunflowers, tulips, gardenias, or roses, marijuana grew sticky flowers that smelled more like the perfume a skunk ejects from the scent glands on its back side than a merry nosegay. Also, unlike its garden variety counterparts, weed decided to broadcast her smell so you wouldn't have to lean in to capture her essence. When driving through Mendocino County in the fall it was not considered uncommon to smell the skunky aroma wafting through the air at all hours of the day. Certainly burned weed produced a strong scent upon ignition, but what most captivated the sense of smell of the residents of the Emerald Triangle were the odiferous flowers in all their garden glory transmitting an undeniable odor throughout the Northern California autumn. While plants and humans haven't had the benefit of lucid communications between their species yet, one cannot deny that anything going to such drastic lengths to be noticed has something to share and a reason to be known.

Indeed, pot attracted the attention of humans, luring them in with her fragrance. Upon closer inspection, humans saw a sticky, resinous plant, replete with a crystalline matrix covering the leaves and flowers. Hairy parts jutted out, visually sparser than our own bodies produce but recognizable nonetheless as a kindred creation. While we may never know by what means these plants convinced humans to imbibe them, we can perhaps give thanks that they were so persuasive.

Midday

Forest rolled up onto the round dead end at the ridge top with a champagne-colored van full of trimmers who had traveled to Northern California specifically to earn some money working the fall weed harvest. They came from far and wide, each having some loose association with Forest so that they successfully passed his pre-screening protocol for the position of illegal migrant worker for the month of October.

Although Forest had not been a part of the growing of the plants at his parents' homestead in Redwood Valley, he had long since become their head of management, distribution, and diversification for the ridge top crop. Soon after Forest left for college he began to be exposed to new strains of herb and new connections with entrepreneurs in the dispensary business through being a young stoner with access to lots of growers. For years he established contacts within the industry so that he could sell his parents' weed in the city. Because Forest was invested in the success of his parents' operation, he helped make sure everything was in place for them by delivering a crew of qualified trimmers to their door every fall.

This year the van held all newcomers on their way to their pot trimming initiation. First off the van were two college kids from Spain that Forest had met in Italy doing a slow foods tour with Marcus the summer before; Lorenzo and Camila were chosen mostly because they were foodies and Forest knew that they would appreciate his parents' place. Next to exit was Lucas, a twenty something farmer from a Steiner community back East who came out West to earn some cash for world travels he intended to embark on after the trimming scene let out. Forest found him interning at a friend's farm, and the two connected when Lucas shared that he was hoping to see a marijuana-growing operation. Finally, the last two on the crew were a couple of queer adults from the Bay Area. Marcus had met Cris and Jo at culinary school. They both identified as avid stoners who hoped to get more intimate with the plant throughout the trimming month; they also were pumped to see Forest's parents' farming operation and had been instructed by Marcus to enjoy as much high-quality food as possible on their work trip.

Most years there was carryover, and the trim crew would come back the following fall prequalified by their previous years of experience and acquainted with the ridge top protocol. This year, however, the crew was completely green. Since the prices had dropped for the sellers in the past five years, the trimmers had taken a substantial cut in pay as well. Two of their usual crew were awaiting the birth of their first child, ready to pop at any moment. Another old friend had been diagnosed with cancer and had moved to Mexico for a year to seek alternative treatments to healing. The rest of the crew either couldn't make it work this year, had gotten a better job somewhere else, or had left the industry to pursue other interests. A job that had once in its heyday, paid $300 to cut up a pound of herbs now averaged half that or less, if the trimmers were lucky to land a gig at all.

Still, Forest had assembled a group of people for the usual illegal task at hand: trimming. He began his introductory speech as they gathered around the top of the driveway, facing him and ready to dive in.

"Weed plants all begin life as a small seed and then metamorphose into a colossal giant, usually taller than anyone in the present company," Forest began.

"Do all plants start as a seed?" Lucas asked. "What about clones?"

"Clones once started life as a seed too," Forest answered. "But at some point somebody really liked the plant that they were growing and decided to make a genetic copy of that particular plant; a clone takes some of the plant's leaf material and uses it to replicate itself over and over and over again. The problem with clones is that they don't offer the diversity of genetics that a garden grown from seed does."

"Does your family grow from seed or clones?" Cris asked.

"We grow from seed. We've always grown from seed. It's a matter of principle for us. But lots of growers use clones," Forest replied. "Anyway, as the seed transforms into a small plant and then into a large plant, the stalk grows, and several arms full of dank herb extend out of the central stalk."

"What is 'dank' herb?" Camila asked, trying to translate the English slang.

"Weed you wanna smoke," Jo replied.

Forest nodded and continued, "maybe it makes more sense to continue this discussion in the garden. Let's have a visual aid for this intro."

The crew followed Forest down the small path to the herb garden. One by one they made their way through the gate, and they marveled at their first sight of the large and in charge ladies.

"These arms are what we harvest and hang to dry. The arms are where the most psychotropic parts grow." Forest pointed to the "Purple Haze" limb covered in colas. "The large outer leaves have to be removed first. Mostly my dad has already gone through and taken them out, but our first step is going to be to go through them and get all the remaining big leaf off. Any questions so far?"

"When's lunch?" Cris asked. "Is that the food garden over there?" She pointed south to where the teeming masses of tomatoes were calling to her.

"We'll have lunch with my folks next, and yes, I'm sure that you'll be spending some quality time in there," Forest responded. "Tomorrow we'll go over how to break down the buds and cut off the unseemly parts to get them ready for market." Forest pointed to the northeast of the garden. "That's where we're gonna be working for the next several weeks. The trim shack has a bathroom and an adjacent hanging barn where the weed is drying. You're gonna get really intimate with that space as you learn this craft."

Spruce and Willow had prepared a meal in the outdoor kitchen. A lattice work roof covered the space, and various climbing plants had loosed their tendrils on the structure, giving it a jungle effect. A wisteria wound here, a grape vine wound there, an ivy made its way across the topmost ramparts, and the foliage offered some shade from the midday sun. They sat down on fir slabs that Spruce had milled for seating on either side of an enormous table made from a slab of redwood that Forest had picked up for his dad from an old barn that had been torn down in the valley below.

"I hope you like pizza," Willow announced to the crew as they arrived.

"We fired up the pizza oven," Spruce said, pointing to the hot coals inside the handmade oven.

"We already cooked up the personal size dough rounds, so the crusts are warm," Willow said, gesturing toward the table full of several small, steaming pizzas.

"You can personalize your pizza with toppings, and then we'll toss them back into the oven to get 'em hot and ready for you," Spruce continued.

Willow had a banquet of several small dishes, all brimming full of delicious contents waiting for the trimmers. Forest started to demonstrate, taking a plate with a ready pizza crust and adorning his dough with his mother's offerings; the trimmers followed suit, heaping delicious toppings onto their pizzas before queuing up to get their pie back into the oven. Herbed goat cheese, fire-roasted tomatoes, sautéed mushrooms, and fresh pestos were scooped onto pizza after pizza. Some home-cured olives had been pitted and cut up. Grilled vegetables diced into bite-sized pieces filled several bowls. Finally, a plate heaped with raw arugula waited at the end of the line.

Everybody sat down to enjoy their first meal together on the land as the trimmer crew for 2017.

"Do you get many really odd personalities in this line of work?" Lucas asked.

"Yourself included?" Spruce joked.

"Certainly, I cannot speak for anyone else and their scenes, but I have always felt that our crew isn't so much a freak show of the motliest characters as much as a reunion of rebel souls. I wonder what it's like in other circles," Willow said.

"We have always had the advantage of having great people come work for us. Forest picks hardworking folks to be on crew," Spruce admitted.

"Feels like a camp-out to me," said Lucas.

"That's because my parents are some woke ass bosses," Forest declared. "They've got their scene down. Welcome to a trimmer's paradise."

"I heard some horror stories about the Wild West trim scenes when I was back East," Lucas continued. "Stories about gun-wielding growers, high action police raids where people had to flee into the forest or be taken to jail, and the occasional story of lousy growers who didn't pay out at the end of the gig."

"We also heard some scary stories about people trimming weed in Humboldt," Camila offered.

"In truth, the underlying principle is that all trimmer crews are random assemblies of willing workers. The common denominator is alternative economics, not necessarily intentional community. Personalities can be difficult and you're lucky if you find a scene where you get paid and can stomach the other folks," Spruce added.

"By the way, don't go over the property lines. You can hike anywhere you want as long as you stay on the map of our property," Forest instructed.

"What happens if we wander off the map?" Lorenzo inquired.

"Our neighbor Ron might shoot you," Forest said, taking a bite of pizza.

"Accidentally or on purpose?" Cris wondered.

"Depends on his mood," Forest replied.

The crew all heard loud gun shots in the background. After a moment's pause, Forest chuckled, "well played Ron, well played."

"That's a pretty sketchy intersection: where pot growing meets the NRA," Jo said.

"Don't worry too much. Ron's a hunter, and he likes to do target practice. I doubt that he would shoot you, but in that regard it still is the wild, wild West, and people would sooner protect themselves and their crop than ask questions and risk being shot themselves," Willow said, attempting to soften the worried looks on the crews' faces.

"Oh, so he grows weed too?" Lorenzo asked.

Willow, Spruce, and Forest all paused. They had an unspoken grower code to uphold, and they were in a bind. Of course Ron grew, and Ron knew they grew too, but they weren't supposed to readily share that information with strangers. A few years ago it would have been more clandestine information, and now, with legalization everybody's lips had gotten a lot looser. Willow sighed, realizing that she had been the one to unwittingly out her neighbor; while she wouldn't normally answer that question outright, she didn't know how to recover from misspeaking so overtly. While she meditated on how she could have explained that Ron was gun happy without mentioning pot growing, Spruce burst in.

"We usually don't talk about who grows. But Ron's gun happy, and it's important not to test it," Spruce covered Willow's slip as best he could.

"When we first met Ron," Willow added, deciding to give more background and hope for the best, "I was pregnant, and we were just coming to the land. His family had been in these hills for generations. He knew the landscape like the back of his hand."

"We respected him for his knowledge of the place. This parcel had belonged to a family member of Ron's, and so he'd had the run of the ridge top. He wasn't exactly thrilled about us coming up to live on the land, but his family had fallen on hard times and sold the property to make ends meet," Spruce continued the narrative of their neighbor.

"The juxtaposition was… difficult at first," Willow said, remembering how they had been appalled by some of their initial encounters with Ron with his gun in tow still treating the ridge top as his own property.

Spruce scoffed, adding, "We were fresh out of college in Berkeley, heady with ideals about spiritual connection to the land. Ron didn't go anywhere without his gun those days, and he took the liberty of brandishing it at every opportunity."

"He kept trespassing for months and would swivel towards us, ready to shoot whenever we accidentally came across each other on hikes. He hunted, but he also had a innate desire and obligation to protect his property. From the time he was a kid, he had been assigned guard duty. Little by little, his family sold off their surrounding plots, and by the time we arrived, Ron was all that was left," Willow remembered.

"We were endeared by his love of the land but repelled by his gun happy manner," Spruce concluded. "When Willow gave birth, I made a point to go speak with him privately about staying off the land with his gun. He consented but vowed to protect his own land under penalty of death."

"He probably started growing around then too, so that he didn't have to sell off his share of the family land. We've tried to be friendly and hospitable, but we're very different people… still, he's in no position to have his crop stolen, and he leads with the barrel of his gun," Willow finished explaining.

"Best to assume everybody grows weed," Spruce replied. "There are a lot of other Rons out there too."

"Everybody?" Camila wondered in earnest.

"No, not everybody," Willow corrected. "But a lot of people. You might as well presume that someone is protecting their personal pot farm whenever you go hiking. It's part of why you came here, right? This area is known for growing and producing lots of pot."

"The Emerald Triangle," Forest interjected. "Mendocino County is at the heart of the largest marijuana growing region in the world. The farther North you get, the more everybody really does grow weed. I mean, by the time you get to Laytonville, it's practically a household plant."

"Yes, we heard on the radio in Europe about the pot trimming jobs in Humboldt County," Camila admitted.

"Really?" Willow and Spruce both offered in unison.

"Yes," Camila reassured while Lorenzo nodded his agreement.

"What did the ad say?" Spruce asked the Spanish trimmers. "Who produced the ad?"

"I don't know who put the ad out, but basically it said that there is work for young trimmers from Europe in Humboldt County," Lorenzo replied.

"But we heard through friends that Mendocino County is also a good place to go," Camila shared. "It seemed to be fairly common knowledge among a certain group. We heard that it was easy to make a trip, finance the cost of the trip, and come back with extra to live on. We heard that there were so many jobs available."

"So you guys and your neighbors and who else grows?" Cris wanted to know.

"We're at the top of the ridge here. Look down. Everybody living rurally from here and north of here is probably involved in the business at some level. Not everybody grows. Some people trim. Some distribute. Some manage farms. Some manage arrangements. The more rural you get, the more likely you are to get more obvious grows. The farther south you go, the more likely you are to get indoor grows which offer more of a clandestine experience."

"We just don't want you guys hiking around off our property expecting that that's okay. Even though the plant is practically legal, fear still motivates growers to do weird things. Stay on our property, and you'll be fine."

"What's the legality currently of your crop? Have you ever been busted? Are you afraid of getting busted?" Jo wanted to know.

"We have never been busted," Willow answered. "But there's always a chance."

"That's probably why there's a lot of paranoid stoners. It's a constant threat looming over everybody's heads. At any point, all of your plants could be seized. The more 'legal' it becomes, ironically, the higher the consequences are becoming for the growers," Spruce replied.

"How well do they keep track of who is growing?" Lucas chimed in.

"They know," Willow replied.

"Who is they?" Cris added.

"They are the authorities," Spruce replied, "and they probably know every grow."

"How is that possible without crazy Big Brother type surveillance?" Jo asked, suddenly tense.

"For outdoor grows, they run helicopters," Willow said, gesturing towards the skies above them. "They fly regularly, and they fly low. There are some grows that are disguised in the forest with lots of other plant cover. They are harder to detect, and so the authorities may not be aware of every guerrilla grow."

"For indoor scenes, they track smart meter consumption," Spruce followed. "If you're using lights to create an indoor grow scene, it's going to show up on your power bill, and they are going to know something's up."

"Is that why they installed smart meters?" Lucas asked.

"Maybe. It's definitely a fringe benefit to be able to track the amount of power being used via surveillance," Willow responded.

"No wonder people get paranoid. They know! They know who is growing and where the grows are," Lucas replied.

"They know a lot about a lot of growers. And as grows continue illegally without the proper permits, they are going to start making this a bureaucratic nightmare for illegal growers. If you don't pay for the permits, you're going to get tagged, and that could wipe out the black market," Spruce said.

"I'm not sure that they want to wipe out all the illegal grows. But I think that they will use that leverage when and where they see fit more and more precisely now that legalization has entered the fray."

"So, Ron over there is doing the same thing you're doing?" Jo asked.

"Ron also amasses a trimmer crew and brings in a harvest. He also has been growing for several decades, and he relies on marijuana to pay his bills. Ron's really not so different from us in that respect. However, his allegiance to conservative values makes for a hearty digression."

"It takes all kinds to grow weed," Willow finally replied.

"There's not just the outdoor growers either," Spruce interjected. "We're old school. We still grow one crop from the summer sun. We trim it and sell it, and that's a wrap for us."

"You mean indoor grows?" Jo asked.

"Yes, both the grows that occur indoors and the grows that use lights other than the sun to grow plants. There's garages all over Northern California full of plants. There's rooms and entire houses devoted to growing pot indoors," Spruce replied.

"Not to mention the light depo folks," Forest added. "They are kind of a fusion of indoor and outdoor growers, and they produce multiple crops each year."

"But your folks just grow the one crop once a year?" Camila clarified.

"Yep. One crop, many strains. This is last summer's 'Purple Haze,'" Forest said as he lit a joint and passed it to his left. "Same strain we saw in the garden today."

"How do you name a strain?" Cris asked, taking the joint.

Forest chuckled, answering, "It's not an exact science. Most of my friends who grow make up names. But sometimes you'll get a seed with a name attached to it and you grow it out and you name your bud according to that strain."

"There's a lot of fruity name distinctions, depending on the flavor profile of the finished product," Willow offered.

"And then there's just the irie name play," Spruce admitted, as he received the joint from Cris. "Take 'Purple Haze' here. That's a throwback to the hippies and the rock and roll free-loving pot smokers of the 1960s."

"There are botanists among the growers. They basically have been taking wild weeds and cultivating the parts that they like the best from them for a very, very long time. In Northern California, this has been a group project — not always cooperative but a tandem leap into entrepreneurial agriculture," Willow explained.

"A joint venture?" Lucas laughed.

"There's basically three main categories of weed plants: sativa, indica, and ruderalis," Willow articulated. "And growers have been taking what they like and growing that out for decades. They've mostly been breeding plants with higher and higher concentrations of THC."

"What is THC?" Lorenzo asked, because translating acronyms across languages wasn't always easy to do.

"That's the part that gets you high," Forest simplified. "Tetrahydrocannabinol is the name of the chemical compound — THC for short."

"Although more and more, the CBDs or cannabidiols are being cultivated and made into medicines too," Willow instructed.

"If you're a botany geek like my mom here, you think of CBDs as the chemicals that the plant makes when the plant is young. CBD production is highest when the plant is mature but before she starts flowering. When the flowering happens, that's when the THC crystals start forming and when they peak, that's when you harvest the plant for smoke," Forest supplemented his laymen's explanation.

"Lots of people only know about THC because that's the psychoactive product of the marijuana plant," everyone nodded as Willow continued. "But CBDs come from cannabis too, even though they are not used to get you high. We actually grow several plants just to harvest the non-psychoactive products of cannabis."

"How do you take it?" Jo inquired.

"We imbibe them. I juice the plants before they flower, make pestos from the greens, and I make some extracts too, in tincture form," Willow replied. "We eat them."

"A tincture is an alcohol extraction?" Camila asked.

"Yes, usually," Willow replied.

"The pesto on tonight's pizzas was made from basil and CBD plant material Willow whipped up in the kitchen," Spruce added, putting his arm around Willow's shoulders.

"But the pesto will not get us high, right?" Lucas asked.

"No, that's why we smoked the 'Purple Haze' joint," Forest smirked.

"A lot of the folks that are studying the rise of the CBD products believe that there needs to be some THC added to the mix to really give the full benefit of the medicine. It doesn't need to be much, but they have something of a symbiotic effect, and the CBD needs some THC to activate it. Right?" Spruce asked.

"Something like that," Willow confirmed.

"Besides, we usually have some THC lingering in our system, so I don't worry much about that," Spruce said.

"Spoken like a tried and true stoner, dad," Forest laughed, starting to get up.

"There's a lot of other constituents in the plant actually, too. They all have fancy chemical compound names as well. But, in my apothecary, I make whole plant medicines. I don't have a lab where I extract specific chemical parts of a plant. I have a garden and a kitchen, and I use my plants to stay healthy by adding them to my foods," Willow said, scanning the dinner table. "It looks like we're all done with the meal. Ready to help clean up?"

The crew followed Willow with empty plates and cups; everybody pitched in during clean up to learn the ropes for their first outdoor kitchen orientation.

Night

"You can all pick your spots. We've got several canvas tents set up throughout the orchard that should be cozy for your stay. When you move in, let me know if you need any more blankets or anything. It can get cold at night," Willow explained. "Each tent should fit two people, and there's some common space in the trimmer shed, too."

"It's clear that you've both put a lot into this land. Does it ever feel weird that it could all go away?" Jo asked, drying the dishes and handing them to Willow to put away.

"In what way?" Willow wondered.

"Do you ever feel concerned about raids?" Jo qualified. "I mean, where I come from, the authorities are always coming after people for substances. Is it like that up here, too?"

"The law figures into an abstracted filter in the hills. It's hard to see clearly and know definitively what's legal. Medical marijuana changed things so that there was at least the guise of legality on the local level. Different states have been legalizing pot, and so there's a sense that even at the state level we're clear. However, the long and short of it is that the law can come take it all away. There are raids. Mostly the feds come in as part of a drug task force to bust scenes," Willow replied.

"Last year there were even some vigilante groups that stormed private property, tearing up weed plants," Spruce said. "It's not clear what's what, and there's a lot of speculation by growers. We're situated at the intersection between free capitalist enterprise and the government's desire to finally get in on a share of the industry's profit. Because we're dealing in drugs…." Willow loudly cleared her throat in protest, interrupting Spruce's digression. Spruce edited his word choice and began again. "Because we're dealing in medicine that the law is still trying to decide how to regulate, there's not a real fixed answer to that question. There's a million possibilities, but most people in our position, running their businesses like we are, seem to make it work. Some people take losses, some heavy losses. The bigger the risk you take, the bigger the potential loss if you do get busted."

"And, a lot of people do get busted. Most of our grower friends are threatening to leave the industry. The cost of having a legal farm entails buying up thousands of dollars in permits for the plants, for inspectors to come assess your garden, and to finance other expensive stamps of approval. With the cost of pot at an all-time low and the cost of growing legitimately at an all-time high, it's hard to imagine that we're going to keep doing what we're doing beyond this year," Willow added.

"With legalization, if you're not in compliance, you can get a hefty fine that will effectively shut down your business. Because the legalization piece is just now happening, we're in a very limbo-like grey area. We figure we've got a couple years in the grace period, at most, while the bureaucrats figure out exactly how they're going to police the permitted grows. Soon though, we'll truly come to the end of the rural weed producing era."

"What about fire? You guys ever afraid you'll get picked off by fire?" Lucas asked over the sudsing splash of dishes and sponges in the sink. "This is my first summer in my life in California, and it's drier than anything I've ever seen. It doesn't rain here for months on end?!"

"There must be impressive American fire-fighting operations, no?" Lorenzo asked. "Isn't the American military number one?"

"There should be," Spruce answered. "But generally speaking, there is not enough funding given to adequate forest management, which is truly required in order to prevent out of control burns."

"Surely you are mistaken? Doesn't California have one of the most impressive economies in the world? Couldn't you finance anything you want?" Camila reiterated.

"Most rural populations have volunteer fire fighting operations. Our fire station in Redwood Valley isn't staffed to deal with large scale fires. They aren't allotted the money to tend the wilderness. Even though that seems like a basic and understandable question that you have, the truth is that the defense of our homeland spaces has not been financed to properly cover the necessities," Willow continued.

"With the amount of money spent on so-called 'defense' we should be seeing troops defend the stewardship of the earth," Cris added.

"Shouldn't there be a working fire department everywhere? Some things should be universally accepted civic guarantees," Jo declared. "For a wealthy, supposedly progressive nation, we should be spending our budget on the things that really matter to the safety of the people."

"Yes, the safety of the people... Jo, are you feeling safe enough?" Forest asked. "I was thinking it might be time for a safety meeting."

Like baby ducks, the trimmer crew lined up and followed Forest out the door.

"Ready for some delicious female action?" Forest smiled, extracting a pre-rolled joint from a tin in his back pocket.

"Didn't think of you as much of a lady's man," Lorenzo joked.

"These are the only ladies I get down with, I assure you," Forest corrected.

"Why are the pot plants female?" Jo asked.

"Botany," Forest said, getting out a light. "The females produce the flowers and the males produce the pollen. We smoke the flowers. We safeguard against the dudes getting their messy pollen into a grow system. If they do manage to find a way, it means seedy weed, and so the ladies are strongly guarded against unwanted male advances," Forest interpreted.

"As it should be," Cris nodded approval.

Forest raised his lighter, "Cheers." After a long inhale, Forest passed the joint. Exhaling, he commented, "sometimes the females do go genderqueer though."

"I know how that is," Jo replied, nodding knowingly.

The joint moved around the circle. A small red coal gleamed as each person took a toke, slowly burning back the hemp paper. As the herb went up in smoke, the group grew quiet, letting the stillness of the nighttime wash over them.

Spruce came out of the kitchen with his arms full of large metal cooking pans, long wooden spoons, and stainless steel pots. "Do you guys have the energy for an extracurricular project on the land?" Spruce asked, his question punctuated by metal clinking sounds.

Everybody nodded, not exactly sure what activity required all this cookery.

"Great! Grab a spoon and a metal piece and follow me," Spruce said, smiling.

The parade wove past the greenhouse and out to a tall willow stand near the pond. Here, under the shade of the willow trees, a pallet stacked high with logs was covered in burlap sacks. Murmurs were whispered among the giggling trimmers about how this might be a training for their work shifts; nobody however, even Forest, had words for what was unfolding.

"Under these wet burlap sacks are oak logs that I've inoculated with mushroom spawn," Spruce started.

"You grow your own mushrooms? I'm impressed," Cris asked, surprised that she had come to trim weed and was now getting a lesson in mushroom cultivation.

"These logs are being eaten up as we speak by shiitake mycelium," Spruce continued.

"Mushrooms are going to grow out of these logs?" Lucas asked.

"Yes. Eventually. Usually there's a rain by now in the fall, and the mushrooms tend to pop up after a good soaking," Spruce instructed. "But with the drought I had to intervene; I submerged each of the logs in the pond, and I'm hoping that all that moisture will help to get the mushrooms going." Spruce pulled back a burlap sack to reveal the stacking pattern of the mushroom logs. "I drilled holes along the sides, put wooden dowels with mushroom spawn on them in the holes, and they've been growing out for a year. In the summer I have to keep them moist so they live in this formation, all pressed together. Now, though, I want to move them apart so that we can harvest the mushrooms easily when they start to really produce. First, we're going to lay them against this rack. Many hands make light work."

"What about the pots and the pans," Camila asked.

"You can put them down for now," Spruce replied.

One by one the crew picked up a wet, heavy mushroom log and placed it at a vertical slant against an A-frame design so that all of the logs were stacked with several inches of space on separating one log from the next. All in all, they placed 24 logs in this manner.

"Great! Now, the fun part," Spruce said. "You can all pick up your metal pieces and wooden spoons. Since we've got the logs where we want them, we can work on setting up the more subtle energetic dimension. You see, shiitakes really like a good thunder and lightning storm to produce mushrooms."

Shiitakes didn't grow in the wilds in Northern California. Thunder and lightning were rare occasions outside a heavy winter storm. But Spruce had developed something of a fetish for these delicious and medicinal Japanese fungi. He was willing to go the distance to ensure his supply of shiitake mushrooms.

"And because we don't really have that in the forecast, we're gonna pretend to make a storm," Spruce concluded.

Slowly, he took a pan and shook it so that it made the distinct sound of thunder rippling through the air. He had a rain stick in his back pocket that he turned upside down, and he continued to coax suggestive sounds from his makeshift tempest tools. The trimmers all looked around at each other, giddy with the permission to both make noise and make believe. The storm started slowly, with one person adding sound here, and then another. As they began to accept their first task, the soundscape reached a crescendo, with everyone contributing to the fitful fury of artificial thunderstorm voices. Different pans added different timbres, and as they waged their blustering with increasing fervor, everyone found a sound and a part in the tumultuous staging. Together, as one, they coalesced into an uproar. Then suddenly, with Spruce conducting, the storm broke, and the different parts slowly completed their solos. Everyone stood in quiet stillness, taking in the expanse of stars that had filled the sky.

"A lot happened today," Forest finally broke the silence. "How about everybody grabs their bags from the van, and I can show you down to the tents in the orchard?"

CHAPTER 6

Saturday October 7, 2017

Morning

As the sun rose on high for the trim crew at the ridge top, the warmth of the light gave way to a steaming landscape as the dew-soaked hills evaporated. The trimmers bundled up in their morning warmies and gathered outside their tents to begin their first day of trimming. Forest waited until everybody was ready, and then the crew began walking up to the trim cabin. They noticed a tremendous amount of feathers littering the pathway.

"What happened there?" Lucas asked as the crew slowly strolled through the homestead land, getting to see their tent village in the light of the day. Their tents were set up at the beginning of the property. When they had driven in the day before, the first visual that they had seen upon summiting the ridge top property was of the olive trees and grape trellises interwoven with their canvas tent village. Now, with the light of a new day, they were beginning to take in the fuller canvas of the landscape of their temporary home.

"Somebody was eaten, I think," Camila ventured, seeing the clumps of different plumage tossed this way and that, denoting something of a battle.

"A fox is the likeliest culprit," Forest concluded, gazing down at the kill site. "The grapes have been getting munched too. My dad said that's part of why they set up your tents in the vineyards — to try to curb the appetite of the local fauna by having a human presence in the outlying homestead areas. Harvest is coming to a close for most of my parents' crops, but until everything's in, everybody tends to come out of the woods to enjoy the fall feast, indulging themselves on our tab."

Grapes were literally dripping from the vines, their sweet juices encapsulated into tiny packets of sugared concord. The olives were in full fruit, decorating the trees with green and blackening drupes that hung by the thousands from the olive branches. As the crew approached the Wilder family home, they could see just what an impressive expanse of sustenance the Wilders were cultivating on their land. As they walked up the driveway path, they were facing the Wilder cabin ahead of them, festooned with kitchen garden herbs and flowers along the front porch. To the west the food garden and the herb gardens beyond were fenced in by more protected wooden rectangles.

"I saw some steaming scat when I woke up this morning," Jo said, helping to offer more clues.

"Foxes like to be stealthy; they usually stay out of sight. But they have an uncanny habit of marking their perceived territory with their poop," Forest explained. "Tables, chairs, trails, anything that they feel might be frequented by others seems to be eligible domains for their little shit gifts."

"Do they bother the chickens?" Cris asked as they got closer to the barn and the clucking hens. To the east the greenhouse and farmhouse were soaking up the first sun rays, awakening the animals and charging up the solar panels on the barn roof.

"If by bother you mean eat, then the answer is yes, whenever they get the chance," Forest replied. "You can ask my mom any and all questions about the farm scene. I think that she'll have you guys doing animal chores this morning. Anybody ever milked a goat?"

"I'd like to," Camila said, eyeing the the does.

"Great, you'll get your chance today. It usually takes a few days to pick up the hand movements to really get your milking groove on. So don't be discouraged if you just learn how to squirt milk willy nilly in all directions this morning; before the week is out, more milk will be in your milking container than on the barn floor," Forest assured her as he gestured with his hands, demonstrating the proper form to squeeze a goat udder. He stretched his fingers out wide; then starting with his pointer and working his way down to the pinky, he slowly curled his fingers into his palm. "And I know my mom's gonna have a couple of you harvesting things from the garden for the meals throughout the day. She might be giving you an orientation this morning around the food garden to familiarize you with the layout and teach you some of the plants we like to eat."

"When I was thinking about the pot growing operations in Northern California on my way out West, I conjured up all these images of gangs and mafia meetings with guns and violence and dramatic alliances being made and maintained," Lucas admitted. "But, I'm delightfully pleased that I'm here and that it's so chill."

"When I was younger, I trimmed around a couple different places with my buddies. I mostly felt like they were good experiences, and I was making good money, so whatever issues I encountered were overshadowed by the economic incentives. But I heard a lot of horror stories from other trimmers about their wildest experiences," Forest shared. "There are definitely scenes that are more edgy, run by more paranoid growers, that do involve racier environments to work in. I've had friends who were working a trim when a bust went down; they had to flee into the woods and hide for a day. Still, I think a lot of scenes are pretty much back to the landers inviting company over for a stretch of the fall, sharing meals, and bringing in the harvest."

"Almost like the Amish getting together to raise a barn?" Lucas asked.

"Almost," Forest admitted.

The crew met Willow and Spruce outside the front door of their cabin to begin their first round of instruction in the ways of the place. The first day always moved slowly, as they spent the hours between waking and sleeping getting everyone on the same page. Less like a drug ring and more like a preschool tea party, ceramic drinking mugs were presented to all the trim crew members. Hot tea and coffee were available alongside slices of acorn bread that Willow had baked fresh that morning. While everyone listened to the day's affairs, they sipped and nibbled.

"You're paid by the pound for the trimming work, but we ask that you do some basic daily chores too. Everybody takes turns working on the land to make sure we feed ourselves," Willow explained to the crew as they enjoyed the refreshments she had provided.

"You can sign up for two half-hour shifts each day, and the jobs can rotate depending on what everybody likes to do," Spruce added. "There's cooking meals, cleaning up, gardening, animal care, and housekeeping. We'll fine tune the chore schedules as we go along and we find out what everybody is most interested in doing."

"You guys run a well-oiled machine here," Lucas commented, taking the paper and pen from Spruce to look over the shifts.

"You'll have days off from all the work too. In the past folks have enjoyed getting to go to Montgomery Redwoods park to see some of the biggest trees in the area. The coast is only a couple of hours away. Ukiah and Willits are both towns not far from here with restaurants and shops," Willow mentioned.

"Generally, we like you to expect to work every day. But depending on how fast the plants are drying with the weather and how much progress we're making, we will let you know when you can have a free day," Spruce added, explaining the trim scene logistics. "It's unpredictable, but we'll usually know the day ahead where we stand for the following day's work."

After snacks were served, the crew was taken to the food garden. Willow instructed them on the botany of the different edible greens so that they could identify what to pick in the garden beds. Next, they each learned how to feed the animals, and a few individuals collected eggs from the chickens and tried to milk the goats at the barn.

Finally, the members of the trim scene were led up to the northernmost building on the property: the trim cabin. The rustic wooden building was adjacent to the hanging shed where the weed was drying and curing in preparation for the crew; inside the trim cabin the trimmers all sat in their own chairs, which formed a circle around the room. Each trimmer had a work station with a table, a lamp, and a few sets of scissors with which they would manicure the herbs. By and large, this would be the domain of the trim crew for the month ahead.

Before the crew really settled in though, Forest took them through an orientation to show them how their work flow would look. As everyone chose their work station, Forest brought in the first bins of the dried herbs. "These plants have been grown, harvested, dried, and are now ready to be trimmed. This is where you come in. Every day, throughout the day, I'll be bringing in bins full of herbs.

First, I'll cut them off the stalks and will place the 'deboned' herbs in a bin in the center of the room. Next, you'll each fill your work tray with those herbs and take them back to your stations. Finally, you will make the buds look their best by trimming them," Forest itemized. "There are different styles when it comes to how to trim weed. Since none of you has ever trimmed weed before, I suggest that you pay close attention right now."

All eyes were glued to the cola in Forest's hand as he held up a beautiful specimen before the group for inspection. A firm green stalk ran throughout the large, densely flowered length of weed. "This stalk is the backbone of the plant. Every plant has one, and every bud needs them to grow. However, we don't want to smoke the stalk, so as much as possible we're going to get rid of it by cutting off the dense flowering buds any time you can see the stalk. If you can't see the stalk anymore, you're golden. If you can see the stalk, you're going to need to keep trimming to cut the bud down to more manageable pieces," Forest said, as he demonstrated by making a few choices cuts here and there until his plant had been dismantled into its most psychotropic parts. "Now, you can't see the stalk, and only the tiny inner stems are holding this bud together. That's step one. And you'll put your stems in a separate bag to be composted or used as mulch."

"What's mulch?" Cris asked?

"More on that later, in the garden," Forest said to keep the pace of his lesson.

Everyone nodded. The process seemed self-evident and the training, although cursory, Forest must have deemed sufficient, because he moved on. "Step two is to go through the bud you have just removed from the stalk and take out all the remaining leaves that are sticking out from the central bud." Forest pointed with his trimming scissors to a few obvious outliers and snipped them off. "When Spruce harvested the plants, he removed the biggest leaves. That's already been done for you. When you see the plants in the garden, you'll notice that there are several large leaves still focused on photosynthesis. Now you're removing the smaller leaves that are lightly crystalled. They can be used for various projects like making edible oils for cooking, or they can be concentrated to make hash. These leaves and the rest of the parts you are going to cut off from your buds are called shake. They go into their own bag too. From here on, the bud that you're trimming continues to need to have the stems and stalks of the leaves removed. Basically, from the top to the bottom of this bud and on all sides you want to shape it by cutting down the leaves that are still jutting out." Forest made a few strategic incisions, pointing out what the crew would be looking for in terms of the botany and the growth patterns of the plant. "Now you have a finished bud, ready to be put in its own separate bag."

"Can we go over that last part again?" Jo asked, wanting to make sure that all the steps had been integrated correctly.

"Absolutely. When we get you guys all settled in today with the first batch, I'll review the steps. And I'll have you each do a sample bud and I'll check to let you know what you missed or what you need to be looking out for. We'll troubleshoot for a while before you really begin to trim the weed in earnest. The first bud each of you trims today you can keep as your souvenir to smoke. After that, everything gets distributed into your stalk, shake, or bud bags. We'll provide you with more smoke, but it'll be from last year's crop because we need to use that up as a priority since weed can only stay fresh for so long."

Spruce and Willow stepped into the cabin together. "Are you guys done with the trimming intro?" Spruce asked. Everybody nodded affirmatively.

"Lots to do, let's get down to it!" Spruce clapped his hands, holding them together and smiling at the crew.

"Before we all really begin to process the plants, we want to have a group ritual to honor the land," Willow said, smiling as she spoke to the group.

"We want you to do a short walkabout through the homestead areas in silence. Listen to the landscape and to the sound of your own walking, and find something that wants to come be in this room with us on our harvest altar," Spruce instructed.

"It can be a leaf or an acorn or a piece of fruit. Anything really that calls to you; feel free to ask permission to take the item, and then leave something of yourself there," Willow suggested.

"In what way?" Jo asked, wondering exactly what they intended them to do.

"It's up to you to intuit what is called for. But you could offer some of your hair or some of your spit or you could pee on the ground," Willow explained.

"As an offering?" Cris asked. "That's kinda kinky."

"You're here on the land for the next few weeks. We're all going to be profiting from the abundance of the earth. It seems prudent to begin our time together with a gift that the earth can use," Willow further articulated her suggestion.

"You could leave a word or a poem or you might have some other intentional way of giving thanks, " Spruce added. "The idea is to be aware of the privilege of being able to be working in concert with the land. We offer up something to the land, and we'll gather our found objects back in the trim cabin where we'll make an altar for our time together."

Every year the trimming crew had different personalities. Spruce and Willow both enjoyed bringing everybody up to speed on their practices and creating a group forcefield for the trimmer camp. The annual harvest amplified the people traffic, forged a work force, and made a temporary community of their homestead. The Wilders meticulously organized their efforts to accommodate the full-time operation, coordinating a team of eight individuals to trim up the product and tend to their other autumn harvest projects. Trimming weed was a tedious enterprise, best punctuated with the other facets of a homesteading operation to enliven and sustain the troop. For the Wilder family, honoring the land marked the true beginning of the harvest.

Camila set forth out the door with Lorenzo not far behind. She walked out of the trim cabin, past the herb garden, and into the bay tree forest bordering the cultivated homestead. She hadn't gotten far when she sat down on the ground. Lorenzo followed her at a distance, weaving through the bay trees until he came to perch underneath the largest bay in the stand.

Camila closed her eyes, letting the rich spicy smell of the bays intoxicate her; she lowered herself down to the ground, her back crunching the leaves beneath her body. Lorenzo looked into the branches, pulling at this one and then that one, letting the volatile aromas of the bay oils loose around him; a few leaves came off in his hands as he carried on, and as he collected them into his pants' pocket he got a strong scent of the bay wafting up. Camila found herself fidgeting, trying to get comfortable on the forest floor with acupressure points being activated along her frame. She sat up, opened her eyes, and her hand darted to one of the culprits. A small, bright green miniature "avocado" was situated just behind her right thigh; another one pressed up firmly into her left buttock. Camila extracted five baby bay nuts in all from underneath her spot and stood up with these in her hand. Lorenzo peed behind the bay that had given him its leaves, and Camila spit where she had been lying. Together they walked back to the trim cabin.

When they arrived, they saw that the altar space had been expanded. A cloth covered a table, and in the center was a vase with several enormous Ganga colas intermixed with other flowers from the Wilder's garden. Lorenzo added his leaves in an array radiating out from the central vase. Camila placed her nuts between Lorenzo's bay leaf pattern.

Jo had left the trimmer cabin and walked southeast past the outdoor kitchen and down along the side of the barn toward the pond. When Jo arrived, the sun caught the cattails, and ze[1] thought these seedy sausages required further inspection. Jo stood at the edge of the pond at a spot where the cattail growth broke open to a gradually sloping shoreline before dropping into the water. Jo's fingers ran through the towering heads of the cattails, which were soft and fluffy to the touch. As the last cattail head in the line stretched up to Jo's approaching fingertip, ze witnessed the most magnificent intersection of human and plant play: the brown cattail dissolved into a swiftly disintegrating cascade of downy white. Giggling like a child, Jo gathered up a handful of the cattail fluff, sang a song ze had written, and headed back to the trim cabin.

Cris walked out of the cabin and past the gardens, past the orchards, past the vineyards, and southward down the driveway. She didn't want to go too far on account of Ron, but she found a large oak tree whose branches reached out in gnarled permutations that called to her to come and explore. Tentatively, holding back a laugh, Cris scanned the horizon line, looking left and right back over her shoulder and then finally decided that the coast was clear for her to proceed: she reached out her arms, wrapped them cautiously

---

1 'ze' is a gender neutral pronoun that Jo prefers to use as a genderqueer individual.

around the oak, and leaned in. She'd never hugged a tree before but felt that if ever there was a time to experiment, this was the place to let loose with the arbor *amour*. At first her arms felt awkward, with her plaid flannel shirt pressing into the bumpy bark. So she softened at the elbows and let the sensation of being held by the strong oak tree guide her to find a balance between hugging and being hugged back. Finally, when they had achieved equilibrium in their embrace, Cris turned her head to the right and let her left cheek softly touch the towering oak tree. She closed her eyes to relax deeper into her impressions and sensations when a squirrel started squeaking and grunting on a branch above her. She pushed back from the tree a bit so she could lean back and look up to see what was happening. The squirrel ran up one branch and down another, moving this way and that. She was wondering if the squirrel was attempting to talk to her when an acorn fell from the branches and landed on the ground next to her foot. Pleased to have an altar item and not certain how the squirrel felt about her presence, she pocketed the acorn and an oak leaf in one motion and began the walk back to the cabin. After a few steps, Cris heard the squirrel becoming even more agitated and aggressive with its screeching. She stopped, turned around, and remembered the offering part of the ritual walk. Pocketing the altar objects, Cris took off her beanie and ran her fingers through her hair several times until she had collected a small selection of her short curly hair. As she placed this cautiously at the base of the oak tree, the squirrel scampered off, and she smiled as she walked back north.

Lucas looked out from the cabin and decided to head north up to the deeper woods surrounding the homestead. Recognizing the oaks, the pines, the madrones, and the firs, he wound a path through the trees, letting the crisp, fresh forest air fill his lungs. He wandered through the woods until he came to a section of fallen trees in a glade at the crest of the property. The morning sunlight streamed through and fell on his face, warming his cheeks. As he looked around to see what else the sun illuminated, he noticed a huge log covered with a plethora of mushrooms decomposing on the forest floor. He took out a pocket knife and sliced off one of the mushrooms along the edge where it connected to the fallen tree. He held it up in the sunlight, looking over its top side. Concentric half circles colored by hues of earthy browns, tans, golds, and even some suggestion of blues covered the mushroom. Turning the specimen over in his hand, he saw that the underside stood out in stark contrast, completely cream-colored. He collected a few more of these "turkey tails" in his pocket. Then he went around to each of the trees and took a few leaves from each. Next, he collected some stones, some pretty pieces of moss, and he selected a large branch that had broken off a redwood tree. He brought the materials to the center of the glade, where he assembled a natural mandala with the items on hand, using the sticks from the branch as a natural border for the art piece. When he felt complete with his offering, he stood up next to his arrangement. Pocketing a turkey tail for the altar, Lucas tilted his head back slightly to let the sunlight shine on his face while he closed his eyes to listen to the sounds of nature surrounding him.

Midday

After that initial ceremony, Camila, Lorenzo, Jo, Cris, and Lucas proceeded to cut and cut and cut for hours and hours and hours. While pot could manifest dreams and illustrious wealth for the trimmers, the work of trimming the crop relied on a sustained monotony to succeed. A trained trimmer, depending on who they were working for and where they were working, could have earned $1000 a day in the heyday of the Weed Rush. But with the market inflated by so many grows, the average trim job stopped being so lucrative; the earnings of the Wilders' trimmers and of those of other comparable grows ran at a pay rate of about $150 for a pound of finished buds. Most people, with some practice, were trained to trim up a couple of pounds of nicely sized buds in a day. If the plants were skinny, they would take longer to trim, and the finished product was composed of lots of small buds. From a trimmer's point of view, the real weed was characterized as dense, heavy, and full of crystal; bigger buds were easier to shape and took less time to make beautiful. The trimmers received their pay at the end of the month; however, at the end of each day, Forest weighed out their trimmed product and kept a running tally for each person on the crew.

Forest bucked up their colas, removing the buds to be trimmed from the biggest stalks. He spent each day with the trimmers in the trimming cabin making sure that everybody had what they needed to ensure that the job got done. The trimmers took their portion of bud to their personal work stations. Sitting there they would each spend a very long time staring into the botanical permutations of the pot flowers, orchestrating precision cuts while they mused on the myriad manners in which marijuana matures. All sizes, shapes, curves, and clusters were represented over the next two weeks. Trimming combined an intensive study of botanical proclivities with a factory assembly line.

"Remember to take breaks to look into the distance throughout the day," Forest said, throwing in his last round of guidelines before the crew hunkered down for the duration. "You can put your trimming scissors into a solution of isopropyl alcohol between shifts. Use a paper towel to wipe them off thoroughly; that both takes off the resinous material that gets stuck on the blades and ensures that you don't get alcohol on the buds. If they start to get too sticky, switch scissors. You can apply a little bit of coconut oil too," Forest said, holding up a small jar, "if your scissors start to squeak."

Willow prepared snacks for the crew and offered gardening guidance and support for any homesteading project questions. Spruce usually worked on creative projects while the crew trimmed, but this year he had defensible space on his mind, and he had decided to spend the harvest timeline investing his energy implementing fire safety measures for the homestead first. Spruce had a list of fire procedures and phases of completion that he'd shown Forest; mostly, Forest felt that his dad needed to keep himself busy. Spruce loved nothing more than a well-executed plan of action.

"Only you can prevent forest fires," Forest quipped when Spruce came to check on the crew.

Spruce shook his head, clearly irritated. "I wholeheartedly disagree, 'Smokey'!" he retorted in jest. "While I understand that personal action can help mitigate the fallout, I believe strongly that a focus on individualism makes this large, systemic issue unmanageable. We need a society that cares enough to fucking take care of the environment."

"Are you Smokey?" Camila asked Forest, curious if his nickname was an affectionate stoner moniker from father to son.

"'Smokey' the bear is the iconic figure of wildfire management for the U.S. Forest Service. Smokey's adage is 'only you can prevent forest fires.' Every kid in America grows up hearing that phrase, " answered Lucas, who had studied forest management in college.

"Some of the fires in the last several years have been from stupidity. In those cases, individuals were largely to blame for mass destruction. But the scale of what we're beginning to see is unprecedented and has so much more to do with institutionalized ignorance than individual human frailty," Spruce countered. "However, your mother and I are rather attached to our homestead, and seeing as the onus of wildfire management in rural communities has fallen to understaffed volunteer fire departments, I believe that it makes the most sense for me to spend any free time I have from here on out to study the best possible solutions for fire management that I can implement and then follow up on them right here on the ridge top."

"They don't have insurance to cover their homestead for fire damage, and so my folks are taking the protection of this property into their own hands," Forest capitulated.

"Is it really much of a threat?" Lorenzo asked.

"It's a huge threat," Spruce admitted.

"Is everybody around here concerned about it?" Cris asked. "I mean, I haven't heard much about it in Oakland."

"Well, when my dad was a teenager his house burned to the ground. They lost everything: total annihilation. So I think he might be ahead of the curve with regard to thinking about fire safety," Forest added.

"That was a house fire. An electrical malfunction started the fire. We drove home from eating dinner out and when we arrived, it was too late to save the house. It was nighttime, in the winter, and we stood outside staring in disbelief as we watched it all go up in flames," Spruce said, soberly remembering.

The crew grew silent for a minute, with only the sound of small scissors clipping away in the background.

Finally, Spruce sighed and added, "Not all of our neighbors are concerned about fire danger. Yet."

"But you think that's changing?" Jo asked.

"I know that it's changing. A couple years back a huge fire took over Lake County and burnt through several towns," Spruce added.

"What?!" Camila exploded. "Several towns?"

"That's the thing. It's not just a small incident here and there. Bigger and scarier fires are happening each year," Spruce explained.

"Why is it just the West Coast? Why aren't the other states in danger?" Lorenzo asked for clarification.

"It rains everywhere all year long except on the West Coast. The clouds open up and irrigation comes out of the sky! But here they stop seeing rain in the spring and often they won't see it again until the late fall. The forests in other parts of the country don't have the same level of drought and sustained dry heat," Lucas explained. "I studied forestry in New York. I'm considering getting my Master's degree actually. I came out to California to earn some cash and see what the forests are like here. I was backpacking all summer, and I hooked up with some forestry students from California to hike part of the Pacific Crest Trail."

"What did they think about the wildfires with regard to the Cali forests?" Spruce asked, curious to see if the students were also concerned.

"They think we're going to see a wildfire epidemic," Lucas answered.

"Why?" Forest asked, still not completely convinced that his father wasn't overreacting.

"Well, the most obvious factor is that we have populated the wild areas with homes that are difficult to reach, compromised by lack of defensible space," Lucas began.

Cris interrupted, "You keep using that phrase; what does 'defensible space' mean?"

"Basically, it's the area that you can probably protect from the onslaught of fire by removing obvious fuel sources," Spruce answered, and then he gestured for Lucas to continue.

"Well, they talked a lot about climate change and how the droughts, the hotter temperatures, and the forests not being maintained are a really dangerous combination." Lucas paused, scissors in hand, and looked up at Forest. "It's not just California, but the entire West Coast that is under threat."

"When you say 'maintained' you lose me," Jo admitted. "Because... maintained by whom? Loggers?" Clearly triggered by the implication that more logging was possibly a good thing, Jo awaited an explanation.

"For lack of a less charged word, yes," Lucas conceded.

"He doesn't mean clear cutting old growth forests. There's a spectrum in logging, just like in most categories of human activity. There's decimating the entire population of an area at one end, while at the other polarity thoughtfulness is carefully exercised when removing select trees so that the whole forest can be healthier," Forest said, briefing them on his understanding of forest management techniques.

"Diseases can spread more rapidly in forests where the trees are touching. The trees are touching because the forests are not being maintained anymore," Lucas continued.

"But they were being maintained before? By...?" Jo wasn't sure if Lucas was suggesting that the modern forest service was slacking.

"By the indigenous populations of California," Spruce claimed.

"Right," Lucas confirmed. "And also the trees cannot get big enough to reach their full vigor if there is too much competition with other trees. So instead of the indigenous people's maintaining the forests, we have wild lands that are now quite dense, literally. Fire and disease spread easily. It's the perfect storm for wildfire disaster. Because we currently don't have small, regular control fires that burn down the fuel in the undergrowth on the forest floor, we now have the potential for mega-fires that rage out of control."

"Fueled by the downed trees and carried by proximity?" Cris reflected back.

"Yes. It's more than that though," Spruce added. "Wetlands are being destroyed to pave freeways, and the abuse of water does not add kindly to the wildfire discussion."

"Last year they put in a bypass just North of here that was hotly contested on the grounds that the road went right through a wetland. Draining our ecological reserves of fresh water doesn't help," Willow chimed in. She had been waiting at the door for the last few minutes of the conversation.

"And that is why Willow and I are going to go install external sprinklers on the rooftops, this morning, thank you very much," Spruce said. "You have everything you need?"

Forest nodded. "Wet houses don't burn, eh dad?"

"If we're lucky," Spruce added, heading for the door.

"Let's get lucky," Willow smiled, following behind him.

"On the roof?" Spruce joked.

"Everywhere," Willow said loudly enough that the trimmers all blushed a bit as she closed the door behind them.

"Your parents seem to have a good thing going," Jo said after they had left the building.

"They make it work for them quite well," Forest agreed.

"Do you think that they'll be able to keep growing? How is the legalization thing affecting them?" Cris asked, getting up to procure another tray full of weed to trim.

"Legalization has its benefits for sure. But unchecked corporate capitalism is probably going to put them out of business. It's hard to say exactly what will happen, but the market is glutted right now, and my sense is that the industries which can sustain larger operations will ultimately make small farmers lives more difficult if not untenable," Forest replied.

"But there are still lots of small farmers that are thriving in the bay. Farmers' markets appeal to a niche of society in which people actually care if their food is produced in small batches using environmentally sensitive methods. Surely there will still be a need for high-end pot farmers doing it right?" Jo wondered.

"I hope so!" Cris added. "We don't need bigger and bigger corporate takeovers. We need to take back the medicine!"

"There are a lot of pot farmers in Northern California. Folks have been growing for decades. It's literally an art form for a lot of my parents' peers. It's what they've known, what they do best, and what they want to do. We'll see. Some of them might keep growing. But they might have to wait a few years for the law to really shake down in order to see what's truly possible. The cost is a huge issue. We used to get thousands of dollars for a pound of pot. Nobody I know is getting those numbers anymore. A few folks might be posed to profit still, but the rates are down across the market from everything I've seen," Forest said, reaching for his spring water.

"It's sobering to hear what you have to say. It seems like such a sure thing, and I didn't even realize that it was at risk of going extinct," Lorenzo said.

"I wouldn't go that far. This plant has been around long before humans, and I think she's done a pretty good job convincing us to keep her around. She's probably one of the top cultivated plants on the planet," Forest considered. "I mean, think about hemp."

"What is hemp?" Camila asked.

"It's pot without the high," Forest summarized.

"Is it the same plant?" Cris asked.

"Related," Forest replied. "They're cannabis cousins. Hemp doesn't have the THC content that pot does. They both look the same and grow the same, but hemp hasn't been cultivated to get you high, whereas the strains of our pot have definitely been bred to achieve a psychoactive product."

"So, what is it used for?" Camila asked, looking at the cola in her hand.

"Well, that plant that you're holding," Forest answered, "if it wasn't full of all those crystals that we all love so much, it could be made into fuel, fiber, or food. That's what hemp is used for. But, because it's got such dense, skunky flowers, we're gonna smoke that shit."

"American pioneers grew hemp to make clothing, paper, and rope and they would use the seeds for oil," Lucas offered.

"Early scouts of the Americas were given to growing their own fields of hemp to be used for a vast array of utilitarian goodness," Forest said.

"And food, too, right? Like hemp milk?" Cris asked.

"Yes, that's a very NorCal perspective, but yes. How about some goat milk and cookies? 'Girl Scout Cookies' sound good?"

"Are you offering us munchie food already?" Cris asked, bemused.

"Well…" Forest said, building the suspense a bit; he thoroughly enjoyed his return to the ridge top each fall where he headed up the trim crew and organized the proceedings of each day.

"I think that he meant the herb variety. Right?" Jo asked looking to Forest.

"I was talking about a particularly delightful strain," Forest answered.

"Then I say yes," Jo whole-heartedly agreed.

"My mom actually did make a batch of candy cap mushroom cookies though too," Forest revealed. "And I thought you guys might enjoy some home-grown goodness."

"They're called 'candy caps' Forest? What kind of mushroom is that?! Are they gonna get us high? This is only my first day trimming," Cris inquired, trying to focus on the buds while getting thoroughly distracted by what seemed like a very intoxicating proposition.

"Candy caps are a sweet mushroom. Kinda taste like maple syrup. I can guarantee that Willow or one of her friends wildcrafted them. They're edible but not psychotropic," Forest asserted. "This is just the first day. We'll save the next level hallucinogens for after you've gotten into the groove."

"Your parents really have food security! Everybody in America used to grow their own food, but now only a tiny fraction even knows how anymore," Lucas affirmed. "I'm loving that we get to eat from the land while we're here. True wealth."

"Food security, medicine security, water security, fire security. They're trying to do it all out here. Thank you guys for helping bring in the harvest," Forest said, scooting out the door.

He walked past the outdoor kitchen to see his folks perched on the top of their house. "A life of leisure made possible by pot farming. Last time I was able to chill out on the roof was when I was in college," Forest called up to his parents.

"Are you getting the cookies for the crew?" Willow asked. "They've probably cooled down by now."

"Yes mom, I'm getting the cookies, and I'm rolling up a fatty too. You guys almost done up there?" Forest asked.

"We've installed the sprinkler system! We should try it out before we join you to get high," Spruce answered, musing on his love of freedom and disposable time to play, explore, and learn on the ridge top.

Forest smiled back, but their chat was cut short by a low flying helicopter that was scanning their homestead. The rotating blades roared, covering up the family's conversation. Arching back their necks, they all watched as the helicopter made one, two, three passes over their place. Snapped out of their trance by the departure of the helicopter to the east, Spruce and Willow made their way down the ladder. They met up with their son on the front porch, where Forest seemed shaken.

"This is the last season," Forest managed to say, almost in a whisper.

"I'll go talk to the trimmers; they must have heard that and are probably freaking out right now," Spruce announced, taking the ladder back to the work shed on his way.

"I'll get the cookies and milk," Willow offered, "And you roll up a fatty, Forest."

Forest nodded and headed down to the cellar to get some herb.

When Spruce arrived at the trim cabin, he opened the door to find the trimmers all looking very pale indeed. "Welcome to the trade," was all he said.

"They were right on top of us," Cris attested.

"Yes," Spruce disclosed. "They were flying way too low."

"Who? Who was that?!" Jo insisted.

"Surveillance," Spruce alleged. "Different agencies, different organizations. They're all looking for the same thing."

"This is why people get paranoid up in the hills growing weed," Lucas disclosed.

Willow walked in carrying a tray of cookies and milk.

"So which is it? Should we be running into the hills or should we be having a stoney tea party?" Cris asked.

"We usually vote for the tea party option," Willow said, pouring milk into saucers.

"Are we going to be arrested?" Jo challenged.

"Unlikely," Spruce said as Forest walked in with a large doobie.

"That's it? Just fire up the joint and let the munchies take us?" Cris grilled.

"That's it," Forest said. "They run these helicopters all season. It's standard procedure. They're keeping tabs. Just because they know we're growing doesn't mean that they'll come after us."

"You can keep fidgeting if you feel like that helps, but the truth is that you have chosen a profession with risks. Not very high risks for you, since you're only here for such a short period of time and you're not involved much in the distribution of the product," Willow challenged, proffering the tray before her. "Cookie?"

"It's your farm. I suppose if you're not afraid, we shouldn't be?" Camila asked. A million thoughts involving her passport, immigration, and being deported buzzed through her brain.

"We can't promise you that nothing will happen. That's the nature of the business venture," Spruce claimed.

"But we haven't had it happen to us," Willow said. "In all the years we've been up here growing pot, we have never been busted."

"Yet," Spruce added. "There's always the potential for something to go down. But, it's unlikely."

"Tell me more about the unlikelihood of our being arrested for involvement with a drug operation," Lucas said.

"We're small. Very small. Compared to other grows we're a drop in the bucket," Willow asserted. "There is a lot of weed grown in Northern California. We're not the priority. We're vulnerable because technically we are an illegal operation, and they could crack down. But if we were to get busted this year, I would be heartily surprised. It's not impossible, but you have to understand that helicopters flying overhead are expected for fall in Mendo."

"So, we should trust you and get stoned," Jo deduced, taking a cookie.

"Anytime we smoke, it's up to you whether or not you join in. If you're feeling paranoid, maybe the best choice is not to go down the high road," Willow declared. "Listen to your truth."

"And if you don't feel like you can handle the pressure of the situation, you are welcome to leave at any point. You're free agents," Spruce admitted. "You're here because you chose to come here. I know it can be scary, but we're a small, well-run, organic operation, and we're in a limbo area around the legality of growing. It's much less likely that a task force will arrive to take us all away and much more likely that we'll be docked with some legalese paperwork saying we need to get permitted or else."

Everyone took a sigh of relief. Nobody had any desire to go to jail that day.

"Seriously, I made cookies! Try them! They're warm and fresh!" Willow insisted.

"And here's the 'Girl Scout cookies' I promised," Forest said, lighting up the joint. "Let's call it a day. We've got some gardening projects and things we can all tend to on the land while you guys get situated. We have weeks of trimming ahead of us. We want you in a good head space when we sit down in this room." He passed it to Lorenzo, who happily accepted.

"It's a vibrations thing. We'd prefer that you work around the plants when you're happy, enjoying yourselves, and peaceful," Willow said. "This is Northern California after all!"

Lorenzo passed the joint to Camila, who seemed relieved to take it and she inhaled deeply. Munching mushroom cookies, sipping milk, and taking tokes, the group relaxed again into the ridge top reality.

"Do you ever think about growing indoors?" Cris asked. "So you wouldn't have to deal with the helicopter scares and the visibility issue?"

"Yeah, we have friends that have an indoor scene and they can generate several crops a year," Jo said, weighing the benefits of a more covert operation, greater financial gain, and increased peace of mind against the outdoor world which Willow and Spruce had chosen as their current employment.

"We have never done an indoor grow, and we don't intend to," Spruce told the trimmers.

"The energy expenditure for the lighting alone in an indoor grow scene leaves an immense carbon footprint," Willow explained. "Why create an artificial sun when there's a big natural one available to shine all summer long?"

"Not to mention that any time you grow something in a room you have to contend with an artificial environment. That can mean more bugs, molds, and potentially nasty fertilizers," Spruce added.

"Right. If it's not organic, you're gonna be taking in pesticides, herbicides, fungicides, and who knows what other chemical cocktail — whenever you toke up," Willow concurred.

"Besides, we have access to land. We're not stuck in an urban environment, trying to make a clandestine profit from our closet garden," Spruce added.

"Which IS totally the case for anybody who doesn't have a back 40 parcel to play with. Most people do have a closet they can free up," Forest added. "I've known lawyers, psychiatrists, doctors, and otherwise successful people who've grown a crop in their garage to help offset student loan debt."

"You're growing a crop right out in the open," Lucas proclaimed, still taking in what he had seen in the garden. "Do you guys ever freak out about that?"

"Truth be told, we used to grow more covertly," Spruce admitted.

"What do you mean?" Lorenzo asked.

"Well, when the plant was completely illegal we tended to grow different plants here and there in the forested areas so that there was more camouflage because we're so visible from the air."

"Although there is still some tree coverage to the gardens and we have the food garden right next to the herb garden, we've grown a little bolder with the medical marijuana initiatives. In theory, we are legally growing medical weed for medical patients in Mendocino County," Willow said. "In the nineties Proposition 215 passed thereby allowing medical marijuana in California. We have prescriptions for friends who have cancer, terminal illness, etc., and we are theoretically their legal growers. We do provide them with some medicine, but we also grow more than the combined lot of them would ever be able to smoke. The law says that there's an allotment of twenty-five plants per patient. If you grow one awesomely large plant, that should keep somebody in medicine throughout the year; that means you have 24 plants left over to market outside your patient sphere."

"But we're realizing that something new and different is going down with legalization, and we're not sure where that will leave growers like us in the years to come. We're in legal limbo, and the government can't get the offices together fast enough to process permits for everybody under the new methods. My friends who are going through with the new legal route say it's a real shit show," Spruce explained.

"And this is probably our last year growing like this. None of us really trust that things are going to be in our best interests if we continue. We're suspicious enough to lay low and see what happens for a while. Then, we can decide what suits us best in the next marijuana paradigm," Forest concluded.

Night

"So now that we're in the garden, I really want to know what mulch is," Cris reminded everyone.

"Right," Willow said, scooping up an armload of grass clippings. "These were tall grasses in the meadows out there that Spruce scythed down to create more defensible space. Until it starts raining, we want to keep as much moisture in the soil as possible. We don't know how much longer we'll have to wait for rain, and the longer the summer drags on, the less water we have in our reserves. You're gonna spread this mulch over that garden bed," Willow instructed.

"So, mulch is old grass?" Cris deducted.

Willow poured the load into Cris's arms. "Anything that you use to cover exposed soil that will then decompose in situ, giving its nutrition back to the earth falls under the category of mulch. A thorough grass layer keeps the soil from getting too hot and drying out. Whatever heat is generated creates a layer of condensation underneath and traps that moisture under the mulch."

"You guys harvested these annual grasses and are using them to improve your soil?" Camila asked, impressed.

"That's very resourceful of you. We were studying agriculture earlier this summer, and our teacher emphasized the importance of generating your own materials," Lorenzo added, genuinely pleased to have landed a job at such a sustainable location to follow up after their farming course. "Even though she said that most farms bring in most of the materials that they will use," Camila advanced, harvesting greens as she spoke.

Willow blushed with pride before she went on. "We aren't just growing weed here. We're growing our lives in this place. We eat food from the farm. We use our excess to create compost that goes back to feed the earth. We've been building soil here since the 80s. We take so much from the land to live that we feel that we must give back. Intact top soil symbolizes true wealth and health to me. While big agro business absurdly fetishizes a monoculture in which they have to continually spray poison to manufacture their ill-gotten goods, we have an organic farm that we have committed ourselves to improving; where modern agriculture favors extraction, we favor reciprocity with the earth."

"Extraction… like hash or dab?" Lucas asked, trying to track her poetic digression.

"No, that's not the kind of extraction I was talking about," Willow said amused, thinking about the concentrated forms of marijuana he had referenced. "We're not opposed to that kind of extraction though. I meant the extractive economics of a farm that takes and takes and takes and depletes the soil in doing so. Adding chemical fertilizer does not carry weight when we're talking about surviving or thriving on this planet. It's a stop-gap measure that was created during the so-called 'Green Revolution' that turned the meaningful practice of agriculture into an industry attempting to utilize the absurd amount of chemicals leftover from warfare. When I said extract, I meant that there are nutrients in the soil that we need to survive, and they feed the plants that feed us; if we use them all up, does our food have deep nutrition anymore?"

"What about on the local level? How extractive is the Mendocino County pot industry?" Jo said, wondering if the small farmers were more sustainably minded than their larger, corporate counterparts.

"Well, to some extent, even we are extractive. We grow weed and we sell it off the farm. However, we mulch or compost the parts of the plants that don't get you high, putting them back into the garden. We try to keep our inputs coming from right here," Willow explained.

"But, if even you guys are extractive, and you're conscious and thoughtful about your process, what does that mean?" Cris asked while weeding a bed in the garden.

"That humanity is screwed?" Jo suggested.

"Well, agriculture in general is a tricky topic. When humans evolved from hunter-gatherers who foraged with a very light carbon footprint to agricultural societies we made a choice that will forever shape our world," Willow reasoned. "I'm not sure that there is a truly sustainable way to achieve an agricultural paradigm in our modern society. But I am fairly certain that our administration of farming methods on the whole could be drastically more nourishing and less extractive."

"Do you think other farmers in the area care about keeping the soil health up and maximizing the effort for a local economy?" Jo recapitulated.

Willow laughed. "Certainly, some of them care. We have a resilient organic and biodynamic farming culture around here. Pot growers come in all shapes, sizes, and opinion pools. There's a fair amount of environmentally savvy weed farmers who got into the industry because they already knew how to grow plants. We're not alone out here in wanting to give back to the land. Not everybody is out to make a product and get their profit; a lot of people are living on the land, tending the wild, and learning how to be in concert with nature."

"That's why we came here?" Forest said, stepping into the garden.

"That's why we came here," Willow said, harkening back to a line she used to say to her children when they were young.

"To play with the earth," Willow and Spruce quoted in unison to complete the verse.

Dusk had arrived at the ridge top. The setting sun passed behind the hills, and the crew finished up their garden session as the night arrived in purples and roses.

"Dinner's ready," Forest said, "except for the salad."

"We harvested the greens," Camila said as she held up a bowl.

"We'll follow you," Willow said as she gathered up some flowers and herbs to add to the salad.

"I saw that you picked out bay nuts for the altar," Willow directed her comment at Camila. "Did you know that you can eat them?"

"They kind of looked like little avocados to me," Camila confided. "But I wasn't going to eat them until I asked if they were edible."

"You toss out the 'avocado' rind part, and you roast the nut meats. They're a delicious mixture of coffee and chocolate flavors. Similarly, they're stimulants. Would you like me to show you how to prepare a batch of bay nut truffles for dessert sometime?" Willow hoped that Camila had a desire to delve deeper with her found object from the land. "Everybody loves bay nut candy."

Cris walked towards the gate where Forest was holding open the door to the path. "I was wondering today as we spent hours making precision cuts to the herbs… does everybody trim their weed?"

"Nah, most small-time folks who only grow a plant or two for personal use let it stay shaggy. Uncut weed still gets you plenty high," Forest described. "It's the for profit market that makes trimmers have a job. We're trying to make it look good. Trimming's a value-added measure that helps the product get sold for a better price."

"I'm just going to run back to my tent to get another layer," Jo hollered to the group.

"Dinner's in the outdoor kitchen tonight," Forest said, cupping his hands over his mouth to deliver his message so Jo could hear him.

Jo waved back, acknowledging that Forest's message had been heard.

"Do you have a salad bowl ready?" Willow asked Spruce as they stepped into the outdoor kitchen.

"You can set the table, Lucas," Spruce said, handing him a stack of plates. "And here's the salad bowl."

Spruce passed Willow a hand-carved burl bowl. She smiled, nodded her thanks, and went to the sink to rinse the greens with Camila. "Spruce made this beauty."

"Is that madrone wood?" Lucas asked.

"Handcrafted on the land. Wanna check out the wood shop sometime?" Spruce asked as he collected a handful of silverware to hand to Lorenzo to put on the table.

"I never thought that pot growers would be such a conscientious bunch," Cris remarked. "But your family really has something special here."

"It's a particular cultural niche that we have up here in the hills of NorCal. There's a lot of growers that care for the land, and the plants are their way to connect with the land most intimately," Spruce acknowledged. "We're one of the lucky ones, too."

"Yeah, there's definitely a whole culture built up around back to the landers growing weed as a subsistence crop. Most of them are well educated and thoughtful," Forest continued. "But don't get the impression that there's only college graduated old hippies in the hills. I got picked up hitch hiking once in Humboldt by a dude who believed Jesus was protecting the earth by circumnavigating the planet in a spaceship with other spiritual crusaders of light. He was also growing pot… it's an industry that takes all kinds."

"AHHHHHHHHHHHH!" Everyone turned toward the southwest of the property, where the trimmer tents were located and started to jog in the direction of the screaming. As they passed the main house, they could see Jo running toward them at full speed, still hollering with substantial volume, "AAHHHHHHH!"

"What happened? Are you okay?!" Willow asked Jo, who was doubled over, catching a breath.

"Bear," Jo pointed back down the path towards the tents, panting hard. "Over there."

Forest ran out to where the parking area crested, and he could see the form of a young black bear who was barreling downhill into the forest.

"I'm okay," Jo managed, almost breathlessly. "I saw the bear and ran back."

"We really need to get a dog," Willow chortled under her breath to Spruce while the crew gathered around Jo.

CHAPTER 7
Sunday October 8, 2017

Morning

"The weather report says we have gale force winds today," Spruce said while putting the tea kettle onto the stove top. "When have there ever been gale force winds up here? We don't live on the ocean?!"

Willow looked out the window, seeing the trees sway and move. They heard the wind whistling down through the wood stove chimney long before the kettle was due to cry. "Doesn't matter, does it? The wind's here now. If it's going to keep picking up, we're going to need to stake the rest of the pot plants. They're almost ready, but the 'Sour Diesel' could put on some more crystal and the 'Train Wreck' definitely needs more time."

"I can tie up the plants while you do the animal chores," Spruce offered.

"Deal," Willow said, giving Spruce a high five before heading out.

Camila and Willow met up at the goat barn to do the morning chores. "Does it get very windy like this much around here?" Camila asked while tying back her hair.

"I don't remember winds like this ever before in all the years I have lived here. Sometimes during the winter in a storm it might get windy, but this is unseasonable and…" Willow said, searching for the right word to complete her sentence as the wind beat at her face, "freaky."

"It felt odd to me to wake up with the wind here since it has been so calm for the last couple days. I wonder if a storm is maybe on its way?" Camila said.

Forest hollered to Willow as he passed by the barn. "We're gonna go secure the rain flies on all the trimmer tents. We'll make sure to stake them down so that they don't fly away. Everybody just finished up breakfast. Now they're getting started in the trim cabin."

"Oh, good idea!" Willow shouted above the wind.

"Whoa!" Lucas said, noticing a huge pile of poop on the path next to the tents.

"Grape skins," Forest concluded, seeing the purple peels protruding from the mass. "Jo's bear must have been having a good snack before they encountered each other."

Lucas nodded, but scanned the horizon across both shoulders before he looked back at Forest and asked, "Stakes?" Forest produced a bag full of stakes, and the guys took turns circumnavigating the tents, securing them from the buffeting winds. "Does this windy season happen every year?"

"Never before. I don't remember a single harvest where we had to contend with winds like this. Sometimes it's raining, and that's a messy ordeal as we have to set up tarps to keep the plants from getting soggy out in the mud," Forest said before hammering in his last stake.

"Tents look secure!" Lucas said.

"Let's head back up to the cabin. You've got another fine full day ahead of you, learning the zen art of herbal bonsai," Forest bantered back.

Spruce was simultaneously staking in the herb garden; he methodically went through the remaining plants that just needed a little more time in the ground. Using hemp twine, he attempted to prop up branches at vulnerable spots where their weight, with the added element of the wind, might cause a break. "They're so close," Spruce said to himself, seeing the dense crystal formation, "they just need a little more time."

"Welcome back to the cabin," Spruce said, entering the trimmer's zone. "You're gonna spend a lot of quality time in here."

"This herb is really beautiful," Jo complimented, turning a purplish green cola over to catch the different qualities of the light.

"Mendocino County is known for its high-quality weed," Spruce said, picking up a sample bud from the center of the room. "The world over, we have had the most committed growers for the longest time."

"That's changing some with legalization; Colorado, Oregon, Washington, everybody wants to grow weed now," Forest said. "I can't blame them."

"But Mendo's still got something special to offer," Spruce pressed the point. "We do grow 'beautiful weed' don't we?" Everyone nodded affirmatively while continuing to study their respective pieces of pot in hand.

"Of course. What is Mendocino County known for if not its weed?" Forest interrogated.

"The basketry of the Pomo people who lived in Mendocino County is considered the finest in the world," Spruce replied.

"Although the Pomo nation isn't just in Mendo territory, there were some of the most incredible weavers anywhere here; colonialism draws arbitrary boundaries."

"Undoubtedly," Forest agreed. "On both points."

"Isn't Mendocino County where the Jim Jones cult got started?" Lucas asked as the room grew silent. "Didn't they drink spiked Kool Aid and start the mass cult exodus thing?"

"Yes. Mendo's infamous for that. We try not to mention that one," Spruce conceded. "We lost friends to that cult."

"But when you hear about Mendo, it's usually because somebody just got some weed from here. Or somebody knows somebody who came here to trim for a season. Or somebody wants to move here because they're a stoner somewhere where it's still very illegal. This is the herbal equivalent of Mecca," Forest postulated. "We've still got the most growers, we've developed most of the strains, and absolutely, we have the best weed."

"Right now, all across Mendocino and Humboldt County too, people are trimming up product in scenes like this. For the next several weeks, there is a collective understanding that the harvest is upon us. All the major retailers carry those trimming scissors you're using right now; all of them profit from the marijuana paraphernalia at this time of year. And when you go to the natural food store, there is a disproportionately high number of people who are not from around here," Spruce supplemented. "It's a relatively small community, and people tend to know each other. In the fall, there's a population boom with strangers pouring in from all sides."

"Trimmigrants," Forest gave the proper vocabulary word. "Especially Camila and Lorenzo, because you guys are from out of the country. But everybody in this room more or less qualifies because you came from somewhere else to this area for a fixed period of time to trim."

"Welcome to our Mendo Culture," Spruce declared.

Midday

As Willow walked along the paths, gathering up loose ends so that they wouldn't blow away, a turkey feather took flight before her, zooming across the side yard. She scooped up some lightweight harvesting baskets and brought them up to the front porch.

"It's like a wind tunnel out there!" Spruce said as she stepped inside.

"We have to batten down the hatches!" Willow remarked, pushing against the gusts to ensure that the door was closed behind her.

"Yes! I was just getting some tea; I'm heading right back out. I'm on it," Spruce assured her, mug in hand.

Willow took off her work boots and left them by the door. She brought her woven baskets to the far end of the kitchen; she kept them on the top of a large apothecary cabinet. Reaching her hand upwards in a stretch towards the ceiling, she pulled down a cord that turned on a warm golden light. She tied back the curtain that hung in front of the apothecary closet to the left and the right, framing her cabinet in between. Finally, she returned her baskets to the top of the cabinet.

Arms akimbo, Willow stood for a minute, preparing herself for her daily medicine tending. Taking a deep breath in, she broke into song as she picked up a half gallon of fire cider and began to dance around the kitchen stirring onions, garlic, ginger, cayenne, and horseradish; she'd been brewing up this tonic every fall for as long as she could remember. She kept singing, but when she'd made a lap around the kitchen, Willow returned the cider to its place on the tabletop of the apothecary. One by one, she gave each of her tinctures a shake and a shimmy. She checked up on her hanging drying racks, funneling a quart of dried flower petals into a jar. She walked by the sunny window in her kitchen next, helping to mix her oil infusions there with a few flicks of the wrist. Usually there would be mushrooms on the drying racks at this time of year, but there had been and would be no foraging hikes until the rains came and the mushrooms pushed up from the moistened ground. Willow's cabinet had a glass window she used to peer inside to the twenty quart jars housed therein, perusing her ample collection; each jar had been labelled by hand, storing wildcrafted or homegrown herbs that Willow used to cook with her foods or make into her medicines.

Today, she opened up the wooden door to the bottom part of the cabinet. She stored bulkier herbs in gallon jars down below. Moving jars aside to reach a container at the back, Willow brought forth a jar with several cups full of bay nuts. "Perfect! The trimmers are in for a treat," she said to herself, realizing that she still had enough of last year's bay crop to make candies for the crew with Camila. The new harvest would come in later in the fall when the bay trees dropped their babies; Camila had gotten lucky with some early arrivals for her altar choice.

Turning off the light, closing up the curtains, and grabbing a stainless steel harvesting bowl for the greens, Willow headed for the door. She pulled her boots back on and opened the door to a cacophonous sound storm composed mainly of the front porch wind chimes acting like cymbals.

"It's really blowing out there," Spruce said coming into the trimmer's cabin. "I think everything is finally ready for the escalating tempest." He walked to the window seat on the south end of the cabin and took off his hat. He picked up a carving tool and began whittling away at a piece of wood as everybody else continued to trim.

"Do you usually carve while the trim crew is here?" Lucas asked, gesturing to the full set of tools on the floor by the window seat. He had noticed carved pieces all around the property since he arrived, and he finally understood how they had come to the land.

"It's one of my favorite pastimes at this time of year. When the weather starts to turn, I love to be warm and inside. Usually it's not so hot when the trimming is happening. We often listen to podcasts and music throughout the day, tending the wood stove to keep warm. This year I'm gonna spend the rest of the harvest primarily focused on fire safety measures. But the weather's a bit much for me out there today, to be honest. So, I'm hiding out in here with you guys until the wind passes. Maybe this wind means that a storm is blowing in," Spruce pondered.

"And if a storm comes in, maybe we'll get some rain, and we can take the crew mushroom hunting," Forest followed.

"What kinds of mushrooms do you find on the property?" Jo asked. "Besides candy caps, I mean."

"Boletes, chanterelles, puff balls, lion's manes, oysters — it's a longer list, but those are the main ones we like to eat," Spruce said.

"Dad. You're saving the best for last?" Forest asked, shocked his dad had omitted his favorite mushroom.

"Matses! My apologies," Spruce interjected.

"Matsutakes are so prized that lots of local folks hunt for them and then sell them to buyers to ship overseas. Mainly to buyers in Japan, I think. It's another cash crop this time of year, but it's wildcrafted, not cultivated. We usually get a pretty good haul right around Thanksgiving," Forest added.

"We find plenty of other fungus when it gets wet. We can teach you how to key out which ones are yummy and which ones will kill you," Spruce smiled as he scraped off a sharp edge on his wooden art piece.

"You guys are really a phenomenon," Cris said. "You're living my version of the American dream out here."

"It's true. I feel like I'm starting to get a feel for your family, and you guys really do everything. And you're free to explore your relationship with the world directly," Jo agreed.

"I can see that it's hard work, but you have really created an amazing place for yourselves," Cris added. "If pot was still able to support people creating their private oasis, I would move to Mendocino County."

"Wouldn't the world be a different place if everybody had access to land? Imagine if you could grow your own food, wildcraft from the same place year in, year out, and keep a small farm alive," Forest said.

"It's the most fulfilling work I've ever known; being up here is my slice of paradise," Spruce affirmed.

Forest walked to the center of the room, picked up a huge cola to buck, saying, "With thanks to our sponsors, the marijuana plant, for enticing hippies back to the land with stoney homesteading dreams."

"I've never given much thought to the back to the land movement in Northern California. I guess it makes sense that people got land so they could grow weed," Lucas admitted.

"Pot is a gateway drug. Before you know it, you've got a garden, farm, and homestead. Highly addictive," Forest said, laughing at his own re-frame.

Willow walked into the cabin, "Can you believe this?!" She charged right to Spruce and threw down the magazine, open to an article she was reading about cannabis.

"What does it say?" Spruce asked, reading the first few lines before Willow erupted into a tirade.

"Big pharma has produced a synthetic form of cannabis," Willow shouted, clearly irritated on principle that the plant would be tampered with by the pharmaceutical industry.

"Isn't that what big pharmaceutical companies do? They take something in nature and synthesize it in a lab, right?" Forest tried to understand why his mom was so upset. "I mean, they're not my favorite either, but why are you so livid?"

"They've only just made it available, and there are already major complications. People are getting sick from the medication!" Willow declared before beginning her argument in earnest. "Here's a plant that we've co-evolved with for most if not all of human history. We have a working symbiotic relationship whereby we cultivate the plant in our gardens, and the plant gives us a glorious medicine from the earth." She paused and then emphasized "From the earth!" for dramatic effect. "We use pot, and in exchange, she gets to spread herself far and wide."

"That's 'A Botany of Desire' stance on things, isn't it, honey?" Spruce clarified.

"Yes. Ganga's a slut in the best sense. And more. Besides having a beautiful working relationship, there's a whole spiritual alchemy at work: this plant opens the doors of perception wide for humans," Willow continued.

"That's more of a Terrence McKenna slant you're taking now, mom," Forest reported.

"Yes!" Willow smiled, realizing that her family had slid into their literary afternoon banter session. "What insidiousness is this? We have more than enough plant material to help make medicine for the whole world! Marijuana is an easy to grow annual, already being grown extensively. It's inconceivable to me they would unnecessarily test fake alternatives on the populace given the deep-rooted practice of utilizing this particular plant for human consumption. I felt robbed on behalf of the holistic plant medicine approaches of people throughout history when I read this rubbish today."

"Is it really all that inconceivable, mom? They want to make a profit from pot, just like everybody else," Forest shrugged as he made his rebuttal.

"Well, as far as I'm concerned, they can go fuck themselves?" Willow announced loudly.

"Is that your official thesis on the matter?" Spruce asked, holding the magazine in his hands.

Slightly calmer, Willow said, "Yes. Also, a soup and salad late lunch is ready. It's too windy to eat outside, so I'm going to bring a picnic in here. Can somebody help me carry in the food?"

"Sure thing," Jo said, following Willow to the wind whistling door. "I need to stretch my legs."

"Still building up a cyclone out there!" Lorenzo exclaimed as the door closed on the raucous winds.

"She's not a fan of the drug companies?" Cris asked, processing what had just happened.

Spruce paused, his carving tools in the middle of an arcing gesture to form a hollow in the wood. "I think that she can appreciate the science that is available with regard to modern medicines. And in some instances I have known her to take over-the-counter medications. But the garden really serves as her pharmacopeia first and foremost. Her allegiance lives and grows there."

"She seemed pretty pissed about it spiritually too," Lucas said. Remembering her words, he asked "what was the part about Ganga being a slut?"

"Pot has been found in the wild the world over; all the continents that people live on have feral weed growing there. She's had the Sadhus of India and the Rastafarians of Africa making sacrament of her body; her frame has been used to make sacred decorations for Shinto temples in the forests of Japan. She's regularly worshipped in California in ways familiar to each of you. She's our goddess in the form of a plant deity," Spruce summarized.

"She's a loud deity," Forest divulged, smelling a terpene rich bud from a jar labelled "Loud Lemonade."

"Is it time for a tune-up already?" Spruce asked.

"Actually, I was rolling a couple for tonight's field trip, but I can roll up another for now if you want," Forest said while running the buds through a grinding instrument. "It's super windy out there though. Do you wanna hot box the trim room?"

"Seems like a time for group consensus," Spruce acknowledged, looking at everyone in the room. "All those in favor...."

"Say, 'high,'" Forest said, amused.

"HIGH," came the call around the room.

As the trimmers cleaned up their workstations, Forest rolled joint after joint. With the product moved out of the way for the picnic, the trimmers pulled their chairs into a tighter circle in the center of the room. Forest lit up the first joint and passed it to his right.

"Counter-clockwise," Forest announced, exhaling the lemonade smoke.

"What?" Lorenzo asked.

"The rotation. It's a matter of principle," Forest replied. "I passed it right and want it to keep going that way so that everybody gets a toke who wants one."

"Ay, yes," Lorenzo understood, taking the joint from Camila on his left.

"I could start another one and pass to my left, but then the person across from me has two joints at once to contend with on the first revolution," Forest said, explaining his method.

"I've had worse fates dealt to me before," Cris said smiling, seated across from Forest.

"I've been wondering what it would be like to be a plant," Camila began. "For me, I think that is the spiritual side that she brings up: I want to see things through the world of a plant. I wish I could impart breath — to cause people to inhale life deeply."

"Plants give off fresh air when they're growing, and smoking weed causes us to take deep breaths after the plant has passed on," Lucas interpreted

"Seems fairly immortal to me. She lives on," Cris said, receiving the joint and raising it into the air for a toast. "To Ganga!"

"She lives as a phoenix flower, rising consciousness up as she turns to ash," Spruce upheld.

"There are few things as intimate to me as sharing a joint," Camila advanced. "It's like we're all kissing each other on the mouth with her as our medium."

"Some sacraments stay even after all we've done to meddle with the world. She's a survivor, and she keeps finding her devotees."

Night

5:00 p.m.

"I'm gonna take the crew to town in the van. There's a show at the brewery tonight, and I wanna show them around Ukiah. We'll be back late night," Forest told his parents as he headed outside to the crew.

11:55 p.m.

Ring. Ring. Ring. Ring. Ring. Ring. "What is it?" Willow asked no one in particular, rousing herself to a semi-conscious state.

"I think it's your phone," Spruce said, turning on the light, squinting his eyes to try to alleviate the brightness while scanning their bedside tables for the buzzing object.

"What?" Willow managed to squawk out after answering the call, looking at the screen she could see it was almost midnight

"Are you asleep?" Forest asked. "You need to get up right now."

"Why, what's going on?" Willow put the phone on speaker so she could get up and still listen to her son's voice.

"There's a fire. It started in Potter Valley about an hour ago. The winds are still crazy, and it's headed over the ridge to Redwood Valley," Forest said as slowly and clearly as possible. "Get up, get dressed, and get out of there. Now!"

Willow and Spruce looked at each other, naked, barely awake. They both paused, considering what their son had just said.

"NOW!" Forest shouted.

Spruce picked up the phone while Willow opened her dresser. "We're up. We're getting ready. Do you know anything else?"

"We're at the Brew Pub and people are talking about the fire that just started in Potter. I called my buddy who has a grow on the ridge between Potter and Redwood Valley. He was awake and staking his plants because of the heavy winds. He told me that he could see flames before he hung up. If it's blowing up the ridge to him, that means it's just one ridge over from our ridge top."

Spruce had started opening drawers now too. "They'll probably get it out though before it gets here. Still, thanks for the head's up son. I mean, I bet there's a team of firefighters on…."

"SPRUCE!" Willow screamed from the kitchen.

"I gotta go, Forest. Thank you. Stay safe son!" Spruce pulled on a pair of pants and beelined towards Willow's voice. As he left the bedroom, he came into the kitchen, where he could plainly see through the kitchen window that flames were coming over the ridge top from Potter. Willow's eyes were glued too.

Spruce and Willow Wilder were not prepared for the vision that jarred them into waking consciousness. When they had imagined fire danger in the past, they didn't ever envision a firestorm coming for them. They had their solid, clear, and dutiful evacuation plans to execute in case of an emergency. They had always secretly thought that they would remain on their homestead and fight any fires that threatened their beloved home; they had fire hoses set up and they had the means to fight the blaze, but they weren't fire fighters, and this wasn't a simple spot fire.

"It's massive," Willow said, grabbing Spruce's hand. "It's massive and it's coming this way."

"It's night! Shit! It's night-time," Spruce shouted.

"What? Why does that matter?" Willow asked, her apprehension growing with Spruce's swearing.

"Because they can't fly bomber planes at night. They could crash into each other without proper visibility, so they don't do it. This isn't going to get better until morning," Spruce said. Frustrated, he began pacing as they talked.

"What about ground crews?" Willow almost whispered her voice had gotten so quiet, her mind in a trance as she studied the licking flames coming toward them.

"No ground crew could contain THAT!? We have to get out of…." But Spruce's words fell short because in the distance they could see fires sprouting up all across the other side of the valley. Explosions blew up in several isolated areas away from the initial fire, one by one starting their own blazes.

"What's that?! Why are those fires happening?" Willow shrieked, panicked.

"The fire from Potter must have hit a transformer and they're blowing up the breakers in a domino effect," Spruce watched the isolated fires springing up and gaining momentum.

With the hillside ablaze, the Wilders had to abandon their fantastic and heroic notions of fighting the fire. Spruce understood when he laid eyes on the scene that he needed to evacuate the property with due haste. Willow witnessed the flames progressing steadily in her direction and surrendered any lingering desire to attempt to personally stop the firewall.

"But, now it's not just the Potter Valley fire. Now, with the winds, the new fires could get pushed into right into the heart of Redwood Valley," Willow said and raced back to the bedroom, realizing the view that they were afforded by their location.

Surrender, implicit in their late night scrambling, washed over both Willow and Spruce. They weren't going to stay. They weren't going to fight. They needed to get out, and their very lives depended on making the right split-second decisions.

"Should we call neighbors? Friends?" Willow

"We have to mobilize now," Spruce said, joining his wife in throwing on clothes. "We can make calls after we secure the homestead."

They both suited up, grabbed headlamps, and closed all their windows around the house. Spruce and Willow took one more sobering look at each other and then out the window before they burst into action.

Upon opening the door they could hear the wind breathing life into the fire, like a human blowing on coals to enliven them, but on the scale of gods. Even though they had their headlamps ready, the nighttime sky was bright and glowing red. They hustled to put on their boots but continued to be drawn back into the overwhelming sensory episode that had taken control of their evening. Seeing the flames in their own valley awed them. Hearing the winds roaring like a pride of lions, breathing life into the blaze, stunned them. And smelling the smoke blowing toward them fostered swiftness in their movements as their nostrils burned hot. Stronger than all their other senses combined however was the intangible sense of fear gripping them, asking them spiritually to consider the immediacy of being alive while implicitly inspiring uncertainty about whether they would sustain their animate condition over the course of the night. Adrenaline, pure and clean, manufactured for them internally, coursed through them as they followed the fire drill steps that they had both practiced before without the duress of imminent wildfire. Finally, they both stood up, boots laced, and ready to carry out their evacuation plans.

"I love you, Willow," Spruce said, his face glowing under the bright nighttime sky.

"I love you, too, Spruce," Willow replied, taking in the gorgeousness of the fierce red flames dancing brightly against the black backdrop of the night.

Together, they entered a time out of time where everything moved very slowly as they began their fire-fighting procedures.

Spruce went to the back of the main house to turn on the generator. They were off grid and had enough power to run their usual systems, but Spruce wanted to make sure that the pump had sufficient juice to power the external sprinkler system they had just installed. He flipped the switch for the generator, turned on the hoses for the sprinklers, and walked the line. Everything worked precisely as it should, and the house exterior started to be saturated by the water spray. Two water storage tanks stood on the West side of the house; one supplied water for the sprinklers to the tune of 2000 gallons. The other tank housed a spigot at the base that Spruce simply opened and let flow out; water began to flow out to the land around the west side of the house as much as possible, and the overflow would head downhill to the food garden where all loose moisture would be duly saturated by the plants and mulch there. He headed back to the work shed behind their house, where he approached the large propane tank housed therein, closing the valve and praying against reason that the fire didn't come that close.

Willow grabbed the "go bag" they had packed for emergencies by the front door, tossing it into the truck cab before turning on the ignition and warming up their rig. After defrosting the windows from the cold night air, Willow drove the truck down to where the horse trailer they used to transport their animals was being stored next to the pond; she backed up to the trailer as best she could by herself and then tried to focus on turning the jack so that the hitch would be ready to be joined with the coupler, but her eyes kept straying to the horizon ablaze with a wall of fire. They had been up for less than half an hour and already the opposite ridge had been engulfed in flames. She thought about all her friends who lived on the other side of the valley as she got the hitch high enough to back up her truck.

"SPRUCE!" Willow hollered, hands cupped on both sides of her cheeks, thumbs perched under her chin. She saw his headlamp light bobbing her way. Having finished setting up the water defense system, he headed to the truck to help her with the next step.

"Help me secure the trailer in place," she shouted in Spruce's direction.

Willow hopped in the truck, and Spruce helped direct her into position. As he finished securing the hitch, Willow hopped back out of the truck and headed to the barn to get the animals prepared for their departure.

Stepping into the main barn enclosure, Willow found the goats all hunkered down for the night on their straw bed. "Up and at 'em ladies! We gotta get out of here! She grabbed leashes from the wall and tethered each of the goats by their collars. Since they were still lying down, unsure why she was visiting this late at night, Willow began to clap and stomp to inspire her does into action. "We gotta go girls! Now!" One by one the goats got onto their feet, vocalizing lightly as they did so. Willow opened up the barn door and was about to lead the goats down to the trailer when Spruce zoomed into the barn past her.

"There's a firewall coming. It's the winds. They're too strong. It keeps heading this way. We need to leave now," Spruce said speaking in staccato sentences while mounting a ladder to the storage loft in the barn. "I'll get the hens in the cages," he continued, orchestrating everything in a perpetual dance of movement. As he headed back down the ladder his headlamp fell on Willow staring up at him. "Keep going," he cried.

Willow led the goats out of the barnyard, leashes in hand. They were used to going on walks with her, but she didn't want to take any chances about anybody running off right now. When she came around the corner, the sight floored her. She gasped audibly, standing in place as she watched the onslaught of flame speeding rapidly down the opposite hillside. On the in breath she found her feet again and broke into a trot, "come on girls," she mouthed under her breath while heading toward the trailer in the driveway. Spruce was behind her, chickens stashed into their cages. Both the goats and hens were secured in the trailer. Willow secured the latch on the trailer door while Spruce jumped into the driver's seat.

"Whatever happens, I love you Spruce," Willow quietly said as Spruce shifted the truck into drive.

"I love you too, Willow," Spruce's mind raced as they crested off the ridge top and began the journey down their dirt road. "Call Forest. See if he can update us."

Willow paused, wanting to call all her friends who lived in Redwood Valley. She wanted to make sure they were all okay, that they had also received wake up calls in the night and were evacuating. Looking out to the east as they begin the descent from the ridge top, she knew in the pit of her stomach that not everybody was going to make it out. It had all come on too fast. It was all too surreal. Their visions of protecting the homestead all disappeared when they saw the elements they were up against stampeding their way.

They had been awakened early enough in the evening to assess the situation before it had arrived at their doorstep. What about the neighbors who hadn't woken up? What about the neighbors who didn't have time to decide what to do? Would people be trapped?

Could people outrun the firewall? On foot? In a car? At what speed? The velocity of the wind kept the firewall steadily advancing. She'd never seen fire move that quickly before. She hoped the wind would change direction. Could it change direction at this point? Would firefighters keep it at bay? As the hillside burned red hot, she surrendered the last of her instincts to protect her home: their lives took priority. She snapped out of her mind's frantic racing long enough to call Forest's number.

1:00 a.m.

"Mom? Where are you? Did you guys make it out?" Forest snapped on the other line. "Tell me you're in Ukiah."

"We just left the property. We're on our way now," Willow responded.

Forest paused, then asked, "Is dad driving?"

"Yes," Willow replied as they bounced down the road.

"Tell him to drive faster," Forest cried, a full-grown man afraid to lose his parents. "Go, now! Call me if anything changes. Got it?"

"Got it," Willow replied. "I love you, Forest."

"Love you mom. Now, GO!"

Willow hopped out of the passenger's seat just then to negotiate the gate to the entrance of their property.

On a regular day, the couple took about fifteen minutes to get down to the valley bottom. From there, they would get to West Road. If they turned right, a road which they had used countless times would get them into Redwood Valley and eventually out to highway 101. If they turned left, the road would go for another several miles before it turned to dirt and went over seven creek crossings. If the road got blocked, people would be using the slower route, even though it seldom saw any traffic. There was really only the one way out of their property. As they went down, Willow realized that they were the last house on the road, and they were the final line of defense to make sure that everybody was awake and evacuating. "Honk the horn," Willow demanded as she got back into the cab.

"Why?" Spruce had been making calculations in his brain, attempting to figure in the variables for a calculus expression that took into account the wind speed, the availability of fuel, and the distance between their homestead and the approaching firewall.

"Just do it! Make sure Ron's awake!" Sure enough, as soon as they started to honk while driving past Ron's house, the lights all went on.

"Shit?! He's still home," Spruce slammed his fist on the wheel. "We have to wake him up, and make sure he knows what's happening. He pulled his truck off the main dirt road and onto Ron's driveway, honking steadily all the while.

Willow ran out to knock on the door, but Ron came stumbling out in his pajamas, rubbing his eyes as she ran towards him.

"Ron, you have to go, right now!" Willow pointed towards the valley below, "There's a fire in the valley and you need to evacuate right now. Is it just you? Is Joan home, too?"

Ron's eyes grew wide as he finally woke up enough to take in the view of the glowing valley below. "Holy mother of God! What the fuck is that? Is the whole valley on fire?"

"Ron, is Joan in there?" Willow asked again as Ron turned to finally look at her.

"What? Oh, no, she's back east, visiting family. You guys were honking to wake me up? Hey, I gotta go!" Ron realized, sobering up to the rapidly firing thoughts racing through his head.

"Yes, get in your truck, we'll follow down behind you," Willow said, turning Ron around toward his own truck.

"Judah! Here, boy," Ron called, and his ancient hound came as fast as he could toward his human waiting beside his truck. Ron scooped him up, secured him on the passenger side floor, shut the door, and ran around to the other side of the truck. Ron turned the key in the ignition but nothing happened. The car didn't turn over. "She won't start," he shouted across the driveway to Willow.

"We'll jump you," Willow said, running back to her own truck. Hopping in she said, "He needs a jump." Spruce nodded while Willow dug through the back of the cab to find the jumper cables.

When they got to Ron's truck, his hood was open. He came running back from his house with a coat on this time and a flashlight in his hand. While Spruce set up the jumper cables, Ron climbed into the driver's seat again, and Willow watched the progression of the fires across the valley floor as if in a trance.

A hearty engine roar erupted from Ron's jalopy, and Spruce and Willow gave each other high fives. "Let's go," Spruce said, retrieving his cables.

"Go ahead, start going down now," Willow shouted above the diesel noise into Ron's truck cab.

"I can't thank you enough; you saved my life," Ron said, weaving past their truck in the driveway.

Spruce backed up the trailer and they began the descent again, this time in pursuit. Ron honked his horn every time the caravan passed a neighbor's home, but nobody else turned on their lights. Spruce joined the honking too but decided that most of their neighbors on the road must have evacuated already.

"I wonder if there were any alerts in the valley? Do you think that the neighbors all got notified somehow? Did they have friends or family call to inform them? How many of them are still sleeping? We were asleep when it started, and Ron would have slept through it," Willow said, her mind racing as she tried in vain to understand the enormity of the situation they presently found themselves navigating.

"I didn't hear any sirens. Maybe they were sounding down on the valley floor? Forest knows about it, even though he's in Ukiah," Spruce shrugged.

"I'm just glad we're going to make it out," Willow said, looking to Spruce.

He didn't reply but kept driving down the road.

"We are going to make it out, right?" Willow asked, uncertain.

"I hope so," Spruce said simply.

Ron's horn blared again. They were almost to the valley floor, and the firewall had grown immense. It was the middle of the night, but the sky was bright and luminous regardless.

1:45 a.m.

"We made it!" Willow exclaimed as they came to the last stretch of driveway before they would hit the paved main road. There were trees on all sides of them, lining the road until it spilled onto West road, also lined with trees on both sides.

"We made it," Spruce said slowly, tenuously, unsure if they had in fact made their way to safety.

Willow looked up through the windshield at the glowing sky. She saw embers the size of quarters blowing through the air all around them, and she began to question just how passable West road was going to be. She'd seen the fire's progress from on high at their property, but they had long since gone under the cover of trees and were just now getting to see exactly what was happening on the valley floor. Spruce continued to remain calm, watching the burning glow grow through his peripheral vision. The fire had arrived before they had. Houses on the east side of the road were ablaze. The flames reached so high that all the trees in the neighborhood at the valley bottom were catching and burning.

Ron turned the corner in front of them just as a tree came down across the end of the driveway, blocking them from following him out. They couldn't take the right path towards Ukiah. They couldn't try out the left path that led to the creek crossings. They were stuck at the end of their driveway.

"NOOOOOOO!" Willow screamed, watching their way out be cut off.

In shock, Spruce just stared at the burning tree; it had about a two-foot diameter, and it had splintered into pieces, all of which were strewn across the road.

Then he said, "I have a chainsaw in the back of the truck. But… I don't think that I can cut it up in time."

"And it's on fire," Willow stated the obvious. By now, the couple could see that it was raining embers and the path ahead was no longer an option. The houses on both sides of them were now under threat of fire, too. "We have to turn around and go back."

"Back to the ridge top? That's a dead end," Spruce said but he slowly turned the truck into a driveway roundabout and reoriented them to head back up the hill.

"We're going to have to drive fast. Let's talk it through as we go. What's our Plan B?" Willow asked, biting her lip and staring out the window. "First: drive!"

Spruce put his foot on the gas, and they began the climb up their long and steep driveway.

"We can take the four-wheeler along the ridge top out of the valley," Spruce suggested, knowing it had a full tank of gas.

"We can, but what about the animals? What are we going to do with them?" Willow asked, looking back to the trailer behind them. "Go faster Spruce!"

"What?! Why?!" Spruce said but slammed his foot on the gas nonetheless.

Willow continued to stare back behind them. A column of fire rising high into the sky illuminated the animal trailer. The fierceness of the winds blowing the fires toward them gave the optical illusion that they were about to be consumed by fire. Willow kept looking back while Spruce did his best to drive at top speed up the dirt driveway. "I think we're okay, it's just such a huge firewall, and it's moving so fast, and it's the scariest thing I've ever seen in my entire life."

"Call Forest. He's gonna be freaking out when we don't show up in Ukiah," Spruce commented, less and less confident that they would see their son again.

"Forest?" Willow called out loud after hearing the ringing stop. "Are you there?"

"Where are you guys? Did you get out of Redwood Valley?" Forest answered. "Tell me you're off the hill."

"We woke up Ron and he got out, but a tree fell down before we made it to West road," Willow updated her son.

"WHAT?!" Forest yelped. "Where are you? What's your plan? Fuck!"

"We're driving back up to the ridge top. We're going to evacuate on the four-wheeler," Willow said, giving him all the information she could.

"The four-wheeler. Okay. That makes sense. If you ride the ridges you can see better than if you're down in the valley. Shit, if West road is blocked by downed trees, where are you gonna go down?"

"We'll have to see about that. The fire... well... the fire has progressed a lot and it's moving fast. We're not exactly sure what we can do about that, but we're on the west edge of the valley and it's headed this way. So, maybe we'll go down to the 101 and get a ride from there? Or maybe we can make it across the valley and out Tomki road at the north end of Redwood Valley?"

"Stay alert out there," Forest said, terrified for his parents. "This is the craziest night ever. There's another fire in Sonoma County. They're evacuating parts of Santa Rosa."

"What? The city of Santa Rosa?! How did that fire start?" Willow asked.

"I don't know. I just know I want you guys outta harm's way. How are you now?" Forest asked.

Willow looked at the glowing background and the embers that were continuing to fly. "I love you, Forest. Whatever happens, your parents love you. You hear me?" Willow finally said.

"I love you, Forest," Spruce said loudly so that his son might hear him.

"Call me when you guys get to safety, alright?" Forest asked, his voice breaking as he said the words.

"Absolutely," Willow replied, feeling her maternal caring shift into gear. "How are the trimmers feeling? Do you guys have a place to stay tonight?"

Forest chuckled. "They're fine. We're at Dominic's place. He brought out a hookah. They're all flying high. We'll have a slumber party. It'll be a memorable night for them too."

Willow giggled in a momentary lapse of empathy before she realized just how dangerous her situation still was. "We're winding our way home." What did home mean now, as they were followed by a procession of flames? Were they leading the way for certain doom, at the head of the parade? "I'll call you again when we have got this better figured out," was all she could honestly offer. Or would she call again? Could she call again, she wondered silently. "I love you Forest."

"I love you mom. You got this! You've got the home court advantage," Forest joked to lighten the enormity of their situation.

"Yes," Willow admitted, although she refrained from telling him about the imagery of great balls of fire whizzing through her consciousness. "Bye Forest," she concluded, feeling the weight of the farewell riddled with complexity and finality.

Willow looked at Spruce. "So, we escape on the four-wheeler. What about the animals?"

"What if we put them in the middle of the pond?" Spruce said, half a smile peeking through his stern contemplation.

Willow thought for a moment. She softened, reasoning that his suggestion had the makings of a sound concept. "On the island?" She replied with her own question, considering the logistics required to accomplish that feat.

"That's all I got," Spruce admitted, pedal to the metal still racing up their driveway.

"The smoke inhalation will be horrible. But the pond's the best place as for them at this point," Willow said, surrendered.

"I cut the grasses down all around the pond; there's not much fuel at all out there. It should be a pretty quick burn around the pond. They can all bed down there for the night. They'll be surrounded by water and that's about as much protection as we can currently offer them," Spruce added. "We can come back in the morning and check on them. We'll have the four-wheeler still, and we're both gonna want to see what this looks like in the morning."

She didn't say "if we make it to morning" out loud. They could both use all the optimism that they could muster. She remembered then that she had tossed the "go bag" into the truck; it was filled with emergency supplies. She rustled past water filtration devices and emergency thermal blankets to find the first aid kit. "Hallelujah!" she intoned, as she pulled out a small tin she had nestled on the front pocket of the kit. "Open wide," she counseled, to which Spruce obliged with a wide-open mouth, tongue tilted broadside in her direction. She placed a small pastille on his tongue and simply instructed, "Suck it." She popped one in her own mouth as well, breathing in and out as calmly as possible while she nursed the lozenge along her palette. "Flower essences for traumatic situations," she said, amused by her own resourcefulness under such extreme distress.

2:00 a.m.

The two humans with the animals in tow bumped up the road in silence, letting the subtle energies of the flower-infused candy assuage their anxious dispositions while the apocalypse crashed down around them. Willow wished she could tell the animals that it would be okay, that they were going to be on an island soon and would be mostly fine. She smiled thinking about the absurdity of their predicament. She wondered about hitching them to the back of the four-wheeler, but she didn't know what terrain they would encounter. If the trailer overturned when they were being chased by flames, that could be disastrous for everybody. She considered staying with them in the middle of the pond; if it came to that, perhaps they would have to stay. The fire was hot on their heels, and the winds were blowing with such velocity that she didn't want to stay and see what would happen. If she and Spruce went to the island, then both the truck and the four-wheeler would be out in the open susceptible to explosion, or melting, or both, and then they would be stranded. If the goats or one them needed medical attention, they would be stuck at the rural homestead until somebody came looking for them. Willow watched a family of deer running across the road, probably figuring out their best options too. Did they have a biological memory for fires? Where did they go when this used to happen? California hadn't burned in such a long time here, did they still know how to respond? Or had it been bred out of them with the colonizers' lack of fire management?

2:08 a.m.

Finally, the Wilders arrived back at the homestead. Promptly, Spruce backed the trailer up towards the pond, and Willow unlatched the trailer. With absolute focus on her next mission, she got the goats on their leashes and led them to the raft at the edge of the pond. They all unwillingly joined her on the raft, bleating a bit about their skepticism for her plan. But when she turned her back and tried to leave them on the island, their bleats rose to deep cries of terror. Spruce met her at the edge of the pond with the chickens in their cages, and she paddled them to the center of the island next. They seemed much more accepting than the goats, and a few odd clucks were all that she heard.

"We'll try to come back for you in the morning. I'm sorry to leave you like this. I love you," Willow said, turning to paddle back to the shore. As she dipped her paddle into the pond, having completed the first part of their Plan B, she prepared for whatever would come next. Immediately, she felt flooded by emotions about the firestorm phenomenon fast approaching all around her. The hot wind blew in her face and her hair tossed about behind her as she watched the lava flow down the opposite hills. Hot magma burned up oaks, firs, pines, madrones, and all the untended fuels of the forest in a febrile conflagration that spanned the length and breadth of their valley. As she stepped onto the shore, she could hear the spitting and the popping of trees being uprooted, wooden homes feeding the fire monster, and the wind driving the inferno ever closer to their own homestead.

Spruce had left Willow pond-side and was desperately hosing down the areas around their house. She could see her fire-fighting companion illuminated in the night by this prodigious lantern of affliction. Holding a thin garden hose, Spruce made his final pre-emptive attempt to subdue the devouring firestorm. Willow came up behind him and put her hand on his shoulder. "Let's go Spruce. The animals are on the island now." He let go of the hose, leaving it where it fell, running down the path that led down the hill to the valley and the firewall below.

They held hands as they watched the fire blaze up towards them for a moment, hot embers landing all around them as they located the four-wheeler again in their disoriented condition. They walked together to the small, sturdy vehicle that was to be their noble carriage out of this pandemonium. Delivering them to safe ground became a more and more pressing and difficult task as enormous embers were whipped all around them by the wind. Willow climbed onto the back of the four-wheeler at the rear of the upholstered seat as the deafening booms of the fire echoed throughout the valley. Spruce mounted in front of her prepared to navigate them across the hills as far away as fate would permit; he revved the engine, it purred to a start, and he flicked the headlights on, shining lustrous beams ahead of them to guide their way on a path they had never taken before.

Suddenly, in the background behind them Willow and Spruce heard a loud splash that sounded like it was coming from their homestead. They passed a family of deer huddled and confused in the middle of a redwood grove. They saw raccoons, birds, squirrels, and coyotes, all running for their lives. Where would the bear that had visited their homestead go tonight? How would the wildlife cope with the fierce winds and hot flames?

"It's all going to burn. It's all burning," Willow said as she saw the valley glowing ablaze below them to the east.

More determined, Spruce maneuvered the four-wheeler up along the ridge top, whipping as fast as he could with only a head-light's distance visible ahead. Traveling north out of Redwood Valley, he wound their ride through forested zones and along steep hills until he found an old lumber road that they used to speed out of danger's path.

After fifteen minutes, they were securely out of the fire zone. Spruce turned off the engine. For a moment, the Wilders remained seated, listening to the silence of the night, holding each other, and breathing together. The stars shone brightly on high through the crisp, clear air.

EPILOGUE

The next morning

Running on pure adrenaline, the Wilders continued to drive north until they came to a dirt road that led up into the neighboring town of Willits. When they arrived on the paved streets of Willits proper, they attempted to call Forest to no avail; their cell phones wouldn't work. They drove up through the town, working their way up to the Police Station on sleepy streets. Wide awake at three in the morning, they parked their four-wheeler outside the Willits Police Station. When they walked into the impromptu shelter, they were both simultaneously overcome by the experience of grace. As they saw their neighbors trickling into the temporary shelter, the overwhelming sense of being alive consumed them. They hugged, they laughed, they smiled, and they shared. Everyone determined that the local cell towers must have burned because nobody's phones were working. They listened to the daring escape stories that poured out of everyone's mouths. Cars had been filing past them for an hour, coming up from the backroads at the north end of Redwood Valley; silently, both Willow and Spruce determined that they would take those back roads into the valley when the sun came up to get back to their property. By 4:00 in the morning, the parade of people slowed to a close. There weren't any more cars coming up the road from

Redwood Valley, and all the mandatory and voluntary evacuees who could get out seemed to have found their way. Although they had all probably lost their homes and undoubtedly some people had not made it out of the fire zone, the mood in the station seemed uplifted by the immediacy of their own aliveness. There were several folks seated who stared awkwardly off into the distance. There were others who stayed quiet, too much in shock to respond to anything more for that morning. However, both the Wilders felt the deep connectivity of their community ties as they waited out the night with so many good friends. The skies over Willits remained clear for the duration of the night; as the first rays of dawn light began to illuminate the valley, it became obvious that the smoke from the fires was indeed blowing their way, and a large grey cloud hovered ominously in the distance. Before there was enough light for them to get busted easily for driving a four-wheeler through the streets, Spruce and Willow hopped back on their ride and headed out.

The alternate exit at the North end of the valley that most of their neighbors at the police station had taken to safety was now legitimately being manned by a police car. As they started to approach their turn-off, Spruce gunned the engine and sailed past the officer posted there. He didn't have time to negotiate road closures. Willow clutched Spruce tightly, smiling as she made eye contact with the officer they were passing. He didn't pursue them, as she expected. Maybe he understood their plight. The road turned to dirt, and Spruce slowed to navigate their vehicle through seven dry creek bed crossings. Feeling the contours of every stone underneath them while they worked their way along the road ever so slowly, Willow had a hard time imagining the parade of cars that had used this access as their means for escape. They had told her that the main road down through the valley had been blocked by the fire, and she wondered how long it would be before they had to go off the road and through the fire zone to make it back to their own property.

The intensity of the fire aftermath took Willow's breath away. Driving closer to the valley, they began to see where houses were missing like tooth gaps in a mouth. Not much farther, they realized that the firewall had come through and taken close to everything along the north end of the valley, like punching the teeth out of the neighborhood in one foul swoop. For close to a mile, there were no homes left. Spruce stopped the four-wheeler so that they could both wrap bandanas around their own faces, covering their noses and mouths for protection from the ash and smoke thickening the air with darkness. They passed a truck frame in the middle of the road burnt to a crisp. They had heard one of their neighbors tell a story about trying to get out on the main road unsuccessfully back at the police station. The truck hadn't been able to clear a downed power line in the middle of the road, had caught on fire, and the folks inside had gunned it until the transmission failed. They had left the truck there, hoping to get a ride in the next truck that passed by, going out the alternative exit; the evidence remained on the road, a grim reminder of just how destructive the fire had been. Spruce maneuvered around the downed line that must have inhibited the truck's progress out of the valley, while Willow prayed that they wouldn't hit a hot spot and pop a tire, stranding them in the thick of this war zone.

When dawn finally broke fully over Redwood Valley, shining sunlight onto the gruesome path of destruction from the night before, the Wilders could hardly recognize where they were. The loss of their neighbors' homesteads overwhelmed them as they passed each property, one by one, burnt to the ground, left in a pile of hot ashes and smoking heaps. In a matter of hours, fire had consumed their world, leaving them with an apocalyptic haze and a community in rubble. The sun, masquerading as a red haze, pierced through smoky layers in the sky, burning away in the cosmos so that they could see the fires before them. The smoke screen that endured after the fire had gone, stuck in the geographic abyss of the valley, visually marked an eerie foreboding of the changes that they still faced ahead. With an uncomfortable certainty, the Wilders knew that they would never see fire or smell smoke in the same way ever again.

They had always known that this possibility threatened them. They had never conceived of a fire that would come on so quickly and leave so little in its wake. Weaving down into the valley floor, they saw houses popping up through the smoke. Not everything had been completely destroyed. A stray home here and a stray outbuilding there dotted the otherwise ravaged landscape for well over a mile. Curious, Spruce wondered why those buildings had not been taken? Had the wind shifted at just the right moment? Had those families created a more defensible space? Had they stayed and fought back the fire when it came to call for their homes? Downed and flaming trees still lined their path as they cut through a neighbor's side yard to get onto their own dirt driveway. Musing on what they had seen, stifling coughs, and wondering what they would find once they returned, the Wilders made the climb back up to their property.

Hanging from one chain, they saw their welcoming sign looming ominously as they summited. "Top of the World Ranch," dangled precariously, covered in soot, on a slowly burning fence post. Immediately, the goats let out a cry to assure Willow that they heard her vehicle approaching. Unsure of how to tend to them yet but grateful to hear them still very much alive, Willow smiled tentatively at the barnyard crew, waiting to be relieved of their island prison. Spruce, however, had driven them right to the parking area in front of their doorstep. They still had a doorstep. Their home, unless their eyes were playing tricks, appeared to be standing fully intact in front of them. Spruce turned the key on the four-wheeler, killing the engine, and they both quietly gawked at their home in awe. Nothing that they had seen on the road home had prepared them to actually have a home to come home to. They both slowly hopped off the four-wheeler, not daring to take their eyes off their home at first.

"It's still here?!" Willow said finally, breaking the silence. "The animals all survived the night, and our house is still here!"

"Mostly," Spruce said as he let his gaze soften to take in the fuller picture. On all sides, everything but the home had been burned.

Willow, too, let her focus move from their home to the larger homestead. Walking slowly towards the gardens, she realized what Spruce meant. The fencing around all of their food gardens had burned, not to the ground but almost completely; a few charred planks marked what had been the former boundary of their food-growing space. Most of the food close to the fence line had burned, probably from the proximity to the wooden fence-post fuel. However, the closer they looked into the garden space, the more that they saw: most of their regularly watered beds had survived the blaze! A few squirrels were munching their greens when they walked through what had been the entrance to the garden; they chattered and skittered off as Willow knelt down to examine the ash-covered kale.

Spruce pivoted in place next to Willow, looking at the destruction in all directions. The splash that they heard suddenly made sense as their water tanks were melted into gross contortions; the ground around them had been marked by the force of fast-moving water when the tanks burst open, leaving a wet trail that must have extinguished the firewall on all sides. Carefully, they treaded onward, taking in the extent of the devastation that had been visited upon the land that they had so lovingly tended. Their pot garden now looked like a patch of blackened earth. The gaping maw of Baba Yaga had eaten all their girls in their prime; the fence that had surrounded them had disappeared into ash, which dropped into a rough rectangle of the crime scene; the hot coals kept them from investigating further. Behind their house, the outdoor kitchen trellis had burned. The long table where they had shared their meals had broken in half, with one end a pile of ash and the other end smoldering along the broken edge. Standing strong, the cob pizza oven survived with an ashen brushing to show what it had endured. Beyond them, they could make out where the trim cabin had once stood from the simmering hot spot that it had become. Every plant from the final harvest had prematurely gone up in smoke.

Hardly a neighbor for miles had a standing house. Perched in their garden, they could see they that inhabited a small topping of green amidst rolling hills blanketed in black. They could still see the fire raging on many different sides, although the smoke made their view difficult to trust. Willow placed her hands above her knees and pushed herself back up to standing. Shaking, Willow looked to Spruce, who came up and hugged her tightly. She considered screaming or crying or yelling, but she couldn't find the energy for that kind of release just yet.

Spruce, through parched lips suggested, "Let's go inside and get a glass of water." Willow nodded agreement, and together they raised their gaze to walk back toward the house. Ahead of them they could both see that the barn had collapsed into a blackened heap, with a column of smoke coming up from the middle of the burn. Spruce started to pull away, but Willow held him tighter. "We have a lot of work to do. We'll put it out after we get some water," she said in a monotone while her words fell from her lips, distracted. Spruce tentatively nodded, and they continued to the back porch.

While Spruce poured two glasses from a jug filled with spring water they had stored in case of water line breaks, Willow took out her cell phone to call Forest again. She wasn't sure if the call would go through, but she felt awful imagining Forest trying to reach them without success. Bringing the screen up to her eyes, her phone lit up with numerous voice mails and text messages. For a moment Willow felt hopeful that if she had enough reception to receive calls again she would probably have enough service to send one out. Spruce put a glass of water into Willow's hand. They locked eyes for a moment and then the phone rang. Just once.

"Where the hell have you been?" Forest picked up.

Willow saw that the clock on her phone glowed the time; it was 6:00 a.m. She paused, and Forest meekly asked again, "Mom? Dad? Are you there?"

"Yes sweetie, we're here. We're home. We're alright."

"You're home? The house survived?!" Forest asked, not believing his mother's words.

"The house survived. But the other buildings all got hit pretty hard," Spruce answered.

"That's amazing! You're alive and you're on the land!" Forest's nervousness transformed into sheer joy. "How bad is it out there? I mean, I can't imagine that you guys are out there right now. I tried to get up there, but they closed 101 in both directions because the fire jumped the highway. I'm stuck in Ukiah."

"It's pretty intense," Willow said, tensing as she looked out the window at the red sun glowing through the smoke. "But we're okay now. We're safe."

"How bad is it?" Forest repeated, voracious for more information now that his parents were accounted for on the ridge top.

Spruce joined Willow in looking out the window at the environmental warfare the firewall had wreaked on their homeland. Staring at the scorched earth and trying to fathom how nature might heal the blackened ground, Spruce tentatively offered, "Maybe we'll get some morels?"

Considering the mushroom that harbored a preference for forest fire, Willow nodded her affirmation to Spruce's optimistic slant on the regeneration possible ahead for the land. She repeated, "maybe we'll get some morels."

The Next Week

For several days, the Wilders kept busy putting out spot fires that threatened to burn what precious little they had left. Forced to stay put on the land, they took shifts both day and night to protect their home from the continuing onslaught of wildfire. The winds did not die down, and hot embers regularly blew onto their still standing house; they both appreciated how miraculous the survival of their home had been given the immensity of the fires. Their truck had survived the wildfires and they considered trying to drive to Ukiah to be with Forest; however, they knew that if they left the property road blockades might have made it impossible to return to the land promptly. While the winds raged on, the course of future fires weighed heavily on the couple, and they did what they could to care for the animals in a makeshift lean-to off the house. Feeding themselves and their domesticated companions with what remained of the garden made it practical for them to stay at the "Top of the World" ranch while they remained vigilant against fire taking their home from them.

All roads leading into Redwood Valley were closed indefinitely, and although Forest pleaded with the sheriff, he was not able to persuade anyone to let him drive into the fire zone. There were of course many rational reasons why the cops were now staged everywhere to stop people from entering the fire zone. Firefighting efforts by land and by air were not completely containing the blaze. Aside from the extremely dangerous front lines, the valley continued to crumble from the fires that had already swept through. Trees harmed in the firewall died slowly and unpredictably. For weeks, the Wilders heard limbs, branches, and whole trees crashing down to their final resting place on the forest floor; hiking in the woods came at a great personal risk for anyone so bold as to attempt to search for missing or wounded animals. Sizzling hot spots sent up small wisps of smoke most of the time, but occasionally burnt vegetation clandestinely smoldered without any real warning. Willow stepped in one such spot on their fourth day on the property, and even though she had been wearing her thick leather boots, her skin bubbled up ferociously where the coals had made contact.

Within a few days, the fires were declared a national emergency, and tanks replaced sheriff's cars to block the roads. Aside from protecting the public from the omnipresent danger of the fire zone, the armed presence helped mitigate the arrival of looters intending to steal from the properties that were still standing. Toward the end of the week, Forest was able to sign a waiver saying that he understood the threat of returning to the fire zone and was willing to risk his neck regardless. He brought in hay, chicken feed, groceries, and high-quality fire masks for his folks. Some agency had cleared the downed tree at the beginning of their driveway, and Forest drove up, quietly surveying all that had happened. He parked his van next to his parents' truck and stood in the center of the roundabout surveying the horizon line. Willow and Spruce both ran to join Forest, hugging him from all sides where he stood. Crying, they all held each other for several minutes, grateful to be reunited at last. Finally they pulled themselves apart a little so that they faced the each other; their arms were still wrapped around each other, they turned and surveyed the valley below.

Spruce spoke first. "Looks different, doesn't it?"

Forest struggled to find any response but an awkward nod.

"It looks smaller somehow without the trees' leaves filling the space. It opens up the view," Willow said, trying not to come off as insensitive. She knew just how shocking this must be for Forest to behold; she couldn't hardly bring herself to truly understand the enormity of the change yet.

"It's so… exposed," Forest admitted.

"Not just out there, either," Spruce said, turning away from the valley. "The whole ridge top got a fire make over."

Forest hesitated before following the sound of his father's voice. Tears welled up in his eyes as he took in the view without the canopy of the forest trees. "It's like a war happened to my childhood memories," he managed to say quietly.

Willow took him by the hand and led him into the house. Spruce unloaded the supplies Forest had from the van to the porch. By the time Spruce was bringing the groceries in, Willow had poured three cups of tea at the table.

"Good, you're back. Forest is just about to share the news," Willow said, putting the tea pot down at the center of the table.

"Chamomile?" Forest asked, smelling the aroma wafting through his nostrils while spooning honey into his mug.

"For the nerves," Willow nodded, sitting down to join him.

Spruce started putting away the groceries, but added from the fridge, "How's the world handling armageddon?"

"I've been really grateful for the community support. I get hugs every time I go anywhere in town. I've truly never seen people be so completely decent to each other," Forest began.

"That's so heart-warming!" Willow smiled, stirring milk into her tea.

"I wish you guys were in town to see it. It's like people forgot to be divided on issues. All across Ukiah, there's an unsaid agreement to not be an asshole," Forest continued.

"City wide kindness? That is something," Spruce agreed, joining them at the table.

"It's revolutionary. Businesses are giving away free things. There's places for fire refugees to get food and clothing and gift cards and… I mean, I suppose it's not enough to really recover if you've just lost everything… but it's so inspiring that people have put aside their regularly scheduled agendas to just show up and be available in whatever ways they can," Forest said before sipping from his mug.

"Are the trimmers doing okay? Are they getting to utilize some of those resources? I feel so bad that the crew just got… burnt out. Are they getting what they need?" Willow asked, concern written all over her face.

Forest just stared at his mother who had barely escaped with her life and then came to find out that she had lost her career, her gardens, and almost lost her home; even Willow, in her disjointed state, was still able to summon compassion for others affected by the fires. "They'll be fine eventually. The trimmers were all confused and disoriented at first. I took them around to get whatever they needed for the first couple of days. Most of them made other plans and left town when they heard that they were out of a job," Forest conceded.

Spruce shook his head, still feeling the sting that he hadn't been able to protect their last crop with his fire-defensible space.

"What about Camila and Lorenzo?" Willow had been particularly worried about their having to figure out how to navigate the wildfire aftermath in a foreign country.

"Yeah, they were scared about what it would be like to be in the country without a passport. But I called the Spanish embassy and explained what happened; Marcus came to pick them up and he took them back to San Francisco to sort through the paperwork. They're staying at our place down in Oakland until they figure out their next step. They'll be fine. It's huge news all across the nation. They have a legitimate reason for needing new expedited passports issued," Forest said, assuaging his mother's worry.

The Wilders hadn't been in a position to help their crew out much since they were under "house arrest" on the land; Willow and Spruce both relaxed, relieved to hear that Forest had made sure that everything flowed as smoothly as possible for the trimmers. Although neither of them could say it to Forest, they weren't accustomed to being in the position of having to ask for help themselves; they were infinitely more comfortable being the ones who helped out other people in need.

"What about the damage count?" Spruce asked, hoping Forest could bring them up to speed on the world outside the ridge top. Both Wilders had been so busy keeping up with their own situation that they hadn't a clue what the fire had been like for people other than themselves.

"In Redwood Valley, they're estimating over 400 homes lost," Forest began to enumerate.

Willow's jaw dropped. Although she had seen the devastation herself with her own eyes, she had not been able to contextualize how that fit logistically into her home town. "That's almost a quarter of the whole valley?!"

"And in Santa Rosa, several thousand homes," Forest continued. "They're still counting though."

Spruce sipped his chamomile, preparing for the next set of grim analytics. "And lives? How many people have died?"

"They're still bringing in the numbers...," Forest admitted quietly, knowing that it would take time for all the missing persons reports to get sorted out and for what remained of the bodies to be properly identified. "But maybe a dozen people are not accounted for from Redwood Valley and another thirty to forty for the Santa Rosa fire the same night."

Willow put down the mug she had been holding and closed her eyes while she asked the question she had been dreading since the night of the fire. "Anyone we know?"

Forest didn't want to be the messenger anymore. He shook his head, tears welling up. "I've contacted as many people as I could think of. Almost everyone has written back to let me know that they're safe. I haven't heard the public release of the names of who they have found yet. But people in these hills definitely died that night trying to get out."

Willow stood up and walked outside, bringing a sturdy bag with her as she departed.

"Is she going to the wailing wall?" Forest asked.

Spruce nodded, "no doubt."

Willow had built a small wall along the far northern end of the property. Whenever life challenged her with grief that could not be transmuted easily, she went walking, picking up the largest stones and rocks she could find along the way. When she found one (or more if the grief was particularly heavy on her heart), she carried her chosen burden out past the edge of the ridge top to a rock out-cropping of large moss-covered boulders amidst the trees. There, wrapped around the outer rim of the place, she had constructed a one-foot-tall edifice from her heart's yearning for peace. Although the wall was born from her felt sense of pain in the world, finding places for her grief stones always comforted her; transmuting her heartache into something tangible allowed her both to ritually set down her sorrows and grieve at an altar of her own design. Willow tied a bandana around her face covering her nose and mouth and set out, selecting stones to carry the burden of the tragedy that had befallen her community. With her bag strap secured across her shoulder, she carried several rocks up to her site. When she arrived at the wall, a deluge of tears wet her bandana and dripped down over her geologic totems.

"What about you dad? How have you been holding up since the fire?" Forest asked his father, tears forming in his eyes between sips of tea.

Spruce looked up at his son, and a single tear wet his cheek before he brushed it away with the back of his flannel shirt. He kept staring into Forest's eyes, trying to find the words to describe just how deeply shocking and painful the last few days had been. Usually an optimist, Spruce struggled to share honestly what they had been through. No matter how he tried to spin it, he couldn't find an angle to explain away their experiences as somehow beneficial. Wildfires were all he could think about. The fires had not taken their home, but their presence in his life had consumed him wholly. Breathing, as a baseline, had become something unmanageable; for decades, whenever Spruce needed to calm himself, he found his breath and therein found his peace. However, the air quality outside made breathing difficult, and the usual aspects of nature that grounded and supported him were all unavailable as chaos reigned. His adrenals raging, lungs rioting, and heart pounding, he had spent most of his time fighting the spot fires that kept starting up all over the property. Burning embers were attempting to finish off anything that managed to survive the first firestorm onslaught, and Spruce had been driven to distraction by these most pressing needs to defend what had been left.

Finally, Spruce broke his gaze, gesturing outside to the smoke and ash world that they had recently inherited. "We've been kept busy on the homestead," he said meekly.

Forest cringed, knowing full well what his parents must had been through. He simultaneously wanted to scream at the injustice of having the whole neighborhood burnt down and to somehow also make it better, easier, and softer for them. He considered asking his dad if he wanted to get high; under the usual circumstances, that would have been a panacea for the Wilder family. But as Forest watched his dad staring out the window, perplexed at the intensity of emotions that were flooding his system, he couldn't see how more smoke would help the situation.

Instead, Forest stood up and walked over to his father. Standing behind his back, Forest put his hands on his father's shoulders and stared out at the ridge top with Spruce. Feeling the tense muscles along Spruce's back, taut from overexertion and compounded by the stress his father was holding there, Forest finally found something to share.

"You know the organic winery at the north end of the valley?" Forest asked, sure that his dad had sampled their wine before. "The first organic winery in the country, I think. It's up on Tomki road. Big ranch. Lots of animals. Didn't we go wine tasting up there?"

Spruce nodded, and then tentatively asked, "Did they… did the ranch burn too?"

"Yeah, the winery's gone," Forest admitted but quickly added, "But you know how they had that biodynamic farm?"

Spruce turned to listen, intrigued at the recurring mention of biodynamics in his field of perception. "Did the farm survive?"

"Well, no, that mostly went too…" Forest admitted, while Spruce started to wonder if talking about the neighborhood's demise fell into the category of topics he was prepared to handle. "The barn burnt down, and they lost most of their homes on that property. However, they had a pregnant cow that was due this week. They had been getting prepared for her to give birth the day before the fire."

Spruce's eyes squinted painfully, bracing himself to hear about more death and destruction. He had solicited the darker news, but he didn't really want to hear anymore. "Did she make it?"

"Yes! She did! And when they got back to the ranch after they evacuated from the wildfires, they found the cow mother with her new calf, nestled in the ashes. They named him 'Phoenix Firestorm' in honor of his tremendous survival story."

Spruce smiled generously, laughing a little even. Forest started laughing too. Soon they were both crying and laughing together, imagining a baby bull born from the blaze.

The Next Month

As the firestorm receded, Willow and Spruce were finally able to leave their property. They were inundated with the fullness of the community experience from all angles. Love showered freely on them from friends and family. Many of their relations, now homeless, scrambled to find housing; when they drove to town, they were struck with the harsh truth that they were the only house that had survived on their road. Survivor's guilt set in too as they learned about those who had perished the night of the fire. Spruce held a neighbor who cried, telling them the story of his lost farm animals who didn't make it out in time. Willow read accounts of people's escapes every day, hearing about the miraculous hand in hand with the tragic as the stories poured forth.

Not everyone had gotten out. Some neighbors hadn't gotten the call in time. Some folks tried to leave too late, and the fires were already upon them. Most people who were unable to evacuate perished in the firestorm. Several elderly neighbors remained in their homes, leaving this world when the flames came. One blind neighbor woke up when his home was on fire and managed to navigate his way down into an empty creek bed where he dug into the damp earth. He buried himself alive and after the fire passed, he emerged from his hiding place and fought his way uphill to the road, where he was soon found.

In the aftermath, the Wilders reminded themselves that they, too, were blessed with survivor's grace daily; they still had a home to come home to, and they had escaped from the fires that night. Still, they struggled and couldn't ever completely accept that they were now living in an ominous haze. Trees continued to randomly topple, leaving burning stumps that smoldered for weeks after the initial fire had passed. Their lush, fertile, and abundant landscape seemed more like a scene from the pits of Mordor than their valley home.

Everywhere they turned grief met them, reminding them of the mind-altering loss. Willow often visited her wall, bringing more stones in an attempt to assuage her anguish. She spent a lot of her day practicing yoga, focusing on her breath, and sitting in meditation. Every day she woke up fragile, unsure how to move forward; she relied heavily on her tea kettle to provide her with herbal infusions to soothe her troubled mind. While usually she delighted in externally processing her emotions with her partner, she found herself moved to a quieter place more often; she couldn't find the words to express herself with Spruce for the first time in her life.

Spruce found himself doing in earnest any and all projects that came to mind. To help him integrate and deal with the losses to the community at large, he slowly and meticulously cleared away the rubble from his own homestead. His neighbors had died, and everybody knew somebody who had lost a home. The neighborhood had been burnt to the ground, and so Spruce moved his grief by trying to set things right again at the ridge top. Deeply humbled, he moved slowly as he dismantled what remained of the outbuildings, fences, and crumbled infrastructure surrounding their home. Tending to the mess of their trim shack, Spruce came to fully understand that his marijuana career had ended. Spared the burden of having to clear his own house site, he spent the month after the fires had been put out gradually doing dump runs. He had to dig a foot underneath the burnt-out buildings to remove the toxins that had gone into the land. There was nothing but ash left in the garden. Spruce carefully extricated all the irrigation lines that had melted and removed the ground beneath them. He completed soil tests several times and removed many layers of their ground; when the final soil test came back clean, he felt convinced that the earth was safe to plant in again.

Forest made regular trips up from Oakland to visit his parents. Marcus joined him, and they both helped in whatever ways they could. Spruce welcomed the extra support on the homestead clean-up, and Willow enjoyed Marcus' presence in the kitchen. While life didn't ever quite return to normal in that first month after the fires, the Wilders' lives slowly began to resemble something of their former engagement with projects on the land.

The Next Year

As the year unfolded and the smoke settled, Willow and Spruce discovered what it meant to start anew. Their first winter on the homestead challenged them deeply. Besides having their careers destroyed more abruptly than they had anticipated, they had to continue living in an environmental war zone while they forged their new beginnings. The land in all directions had been burnt, and a stark, bare landscape remained. Even where there were trees still standing, the defoliated branches marked just how drastic the metamorphosis had been; places where one could formerly see a dense wood were now wide open, making distance visible in a peculiarly open way. Exposed, their home sat in full view of the rest of the world. Before the fires it had been nestled into rich woodland, cozy with thick forests; now naked, the ridge top welcomed the first rains over her wounded form. More and more rains came, and with them they washed away some of the bleakness and blackness from the landscape.

Spruce did everything he could to stop the erosion on their homestead. Without the tree, shrub, and grass roots to hold the land in place, they were uneasy about how the storms that came would affect them. Willow shifted her practice from carrying stones to the wailing wall to broadcasting wildflower seeds in the meadows and grasslands. Spruce downed trees that were thoroughly dead, forming weaving wildlife corridors on the contour of the land; with the help of a neighbor with a mill, he processed some of the wood that could be used and donated the boards to families rebuilding their homes. Willow put in the biggest cover crop that the garden space had ever seen. Spruce added mushroom spawn to the beds to help support the regeneration of the earth substrate. They both started learning biodynamic methods with John to help give their garden new life and they began applying all of the biodynamic preparations they were learning about to help rebuild their soil ecology.

Tanya, whose property had survived the fires, spearheaded an acorn bank to help reforest the land with oak trees; she facilitated the collection of all kinds of oaks across Mendocino County as the trees dropped their seeds following the fires. Willow planted a nursery of baby oaks on the ridge top and also helped in the replanting efforts of her valley neighbors.

Ron, who lost his home in the fires, got a trailer and moved back to the land to attempt to start over. Without insurance, without a weed crop, and with most of his neighbors focused on rebuilding their own homes, he struggled to find his way. Eventually, finances forced him to put his property on the market after a difficult winter. Like Ron, several of the Wilder's neighbors were hit hard by the destruction of their family homes. Having one's own house burn down as a fluke event was tragic enough. But Ron's plight became insurmountable because the very people who would have helped him rebuild were faced with the same difficult situation.

Still the Wilders managed to make their way through the winter, cleaning up their home site and letting the waves of grief wash over them. They watched as the rains gave new life to the land, inspired that they too would be reinventing themselves. Bay trees, manzanitas, and redwoods all performed phoenix initiation rites, wherein the burnt and ashen remains gave way to new stems, shoots, and roots. California, after all, had been designed to burn. The forests were thinned by flame. The canopies that were previously overgrown and dense opened up to allow more sunlight to penetrate through. New seeds were able to take root that before had been previously denied space on the forest floor. Diseases and pests across the forest were eradicated in a period of hours.

However, Spruce felt the call to tend to the wilds around him more strongly than ever. California had evolved with fire, but it had also been carefully cultivated by indigenous hands. Spruce, lacking a knowledge base that would truly prepare him for the work that the land needed, created a naturalist study program to bring forth more savvy individuals who could educate his community on this topic; he hoped that the program would enliven conversations and perhaps root out almost forgotten wisdom about what cohabitation with fire could look like in California's hills, valleys, woodlands, and meadows.

By the spring, a new Northern California had begun to emerge. The army corps of engineers had removed most of the toxic waste that littered former house sites. The cost of destruction to homes had been immense, and the burnt remains of homesteads were largely too toxic for people to deal with by themselves. The Wilders marveled at the workers in white suits that arrived all across the valley to take away the burnt blenders and all the modern refuse generated from the firestorm. Whenever they began to talk about where the dump truck loads of noxious debris were going, the Wilders shook their heads in dismay. In a short period of time, humans had gotten so removed from the natural world that their property couldn't just go back to the earth. Knowing that throwing something "away" doesn't remove it from the earth bubble, the Wilders accepted the "clean-up" with a sense of tragic obligation. With the land cleared of the physical remains of the fire path, many of their neighbors started the rebuilding process in earnest. While nobody invested in a structure that could biodegrade of its own accord, several landowners did find contractors who were willing to use fire-resistant materials, which were far more appropriate for a home built in fire-prone Northern California.

Wildflowers flourished as the spring sun shone, honoring timeless cycles on the land. Bulbs burst up in Willow's front yard, and the Wilder's own flower progeny, Lily, returned from her travels to help her parents navigate the post-fire phase of their lives. Lily purchased a tiny house and she had it moved to the ridge top early in the spring so that she could join her parents in figuring out how to repair their homestead, sustain themselves in the aftermath of the fire, and utilize their golden years in the service of their greatest desires for social justice.

Forest and Lily had a tearful reunion wherein they both cried and held each other while they lamented the loss of their stomping grounds; while their own home had survived, their old haunts and the places that they had frequented as kids had all been transformed or destroyed by the flames. Spruce and Willow joined their kids in several hearty cries as well; they gave thanks that they had survived, but they cried whenever they allowed themselves to take the time to process their deep-seated layers of grief.

Lily continued her nonprofit work as an agent for social change on her childhood stomping grounds. Despite her anguish at seeing her childhood memories tarnished by fire, Lily had developed something of a thick skin for helping communities displaced by warfare; she hadn't expected to use her skill set for her parents' homestead or for environmental warfare, but her expertise in grant writing proved invaluable in helping her folks navigate the post-fire idiom. And Willow and Spruce started odd jobs to help them recover without the influx of income from marijuana money. Lily acted as their advocate in all manners pertaining to establishing a new career path.

The Wilders spent their free time together brainstorming and researching how to move forward. Spruce and Willow wanted to maintain their connection to the land and also earn their living in the same stride. For the first time in their lives, the Wilders saw how easy it could be to prioritize making ends meet rather than stewarding the land where they lived. Whereas their privilege had blinded them before the fire, the removal of the pot economy that had subsidized their livelihood forced them to reconcile the struggle that they and most Americans faced: to be a part of a landscape, the requisite cost of participation was wealth. However, where the costs for their neighbor Ron had been too high, the Wilders had buried enough funds to keep them afloat financially through their fire hardships for the first year.

Spruce began interning with his farmer friend John to learn biodynamic methods for their farmstead. Figuring that a niche market could help them pay the bills while being at home too, Willow expanded their garden space to allow for greater production at the "Top of the World" ranch. Forest and Marcus moved forward with their plans to open a restaurant in the city, and Lily helped them establish and market a farm-to-table connection with their folks, using some of the produce from the ridge top in their menus.

The first dry summer weighed heavily on Spruce and Willow beyond anything that they had delved into with all the previous layers of grief combined. The Wilders lived through another summer of firestorms raging in California, watching the fires come close again, and breathing in the smoky air once more. They viscerally relived their own firestorm experience through the Carr fire, the Mendocino Complex fire (the River and Ranch fires, respectively), and the Camp fire. Northern California continued to burn up over the course of the following summer. Southern California, Oregon, Washington, and Canada soon were also burning. The ubiquitous smoke all along the West coast required them to summon near impossible strength when they were still very much moving through the rehabilitation process for fire trauma victims. Wildfires, no matter how many therapy sessions the went to, were inflammatory triggers for their physical and emotional well-being.

The continuous intensity of the rural wildfires created sleep trouble at night for Willow, who developed insomnia for the first time in her life. Unable to fall asleep for fear of fire, Willow would regularly get up, scan the horizon for bright red flames, and sniff the air to make sure that they weren't in danger. When the fire smoke blew in from other areas, it clouded their ridge top vista and they couldn't reasonably be sure that they weren't under threat without a clear view. Even when they could see, the sights were unsettling; after Spruce spent several days watching mushroom clouds of smoke burn over the Mendocino National Forest he took to regularly watering down the land all around the house. The smell of fires became synonymous in their minds with catastrophe, and the Wilders endured the entire summer season very much on edge about their precarious hold on the land. This time, however, they thought there wasn't enough fuel to burn a firestorm even though the constant threat still hung in the hot, dry air. They were moderately safe, they reasoned, despite their traumatized perceptions that aroused suspicious thoughts to the contrary. When the city of Paradise burnt down a little over a year after their own firestorm, the sky at noon grew so dark with smoke that the Wilders suspected an errant eclipse; it became increasingly difficult to sort through these new bits of evidence as their own harried escape played out relentlessly in their mind's eye.

Although Spruce and Willow held tightly to their dreams for the land, they both bawled like babies when images of skinny bears, unable to forage for food in the aftermath of the Redwood Valley fires, went viral; even the strong, top of the food chain predators had to contend with starvation to survive in the destruction zone. Rebuilding efforts became bittersweet in their minds as homes went up without anyone really addressing the underlying causes of the fires. Heartbroken, Spruce speculated that the fires marked the downfall of the "empire" and the beginning of an era of climate chaos catastrophes for the Western expanse of North America. Willow, a year out, agreed that the hardship had not passed; they had not returned to a normal state of affairs, and the confusion about how to personally and collectively transition to a more sustainable model of livelihood weighed on them daily without resolution. And the fires keep coming.